BEYOND AUTHORITY
MANAGING TEAMS IN A RAPIDLY CHANGING WORLD

NAKEL W. A. NIKIEMA

© **Copyright 2025 - All rights reserved.**

The content contained within this book may not be reproduced, duplicated or transmitted without direct written permission from the author or the publisher.

Under no circumstances will any blame or legal responsibility be held against the publisher, or author, for any damages, reparation, or monetary loss due to the information contained within this book, either directly or indirectly.

Legal Notice:

This book is copyright protected. It is only for personal use. You cannot amend, distribute, sell, use, quote or paraphrase any part, or the content within this book, without the consent of the author or publisher.

Disclaimer Notice:

Please note the information contained within this document is for educational and entertainment purposes only. All effort has been executed to present accurate, up to date, reliable, complete information. No warranties of any kind are declared or implied. Readers acknowledge that the author is not engaged in the rendering of legal, financial, medical or professional advice. The content within this book has been derived from various sources. Please consult a licensed professional before attempting any techniques outlined in this book.

By reading this document, the reader agrees that under no circumstances is the author responsible for any losses, direct or indirect, that are incurred as a result of the use of the information contained within this document, including, but not limited to, errors, omissions, or inaccuracies.

CONTENTS

Introduction   9

Part I
RETHINKING LEADERSHIP IN A CHANGING WORLD

1. THE NEW LEADERSHIP PARADIGM   17
   Thriving Beyond Authority
   The Shift From Control-Based to Influence-Driven Leadership   18
   Why Adaptability Matters More Than Rigid Power   22
   The Curious Case of Leaders Who Thrive Without Authority: Some Case Studies   26
   Applying the New Leadership Paradigm   29
   Call to Action   32

2. LEADING WITH INFLUENCE   33
   The Art of Trust and Credibility
   Authority vs True Leadership: Understanding the Difference   34
   Building Trust: The Foundation of Leadership Influence   37
   Influence Techniques for Effective Leadership   42
   Overcoming Common Influence Barriers   47
   Call to Action   49

3. VISION, RESILIENCE, AND EMPATHY   51
   The Core Leadership Trio
   Vision: Leading With Clarity in Uncertain Times   52
   Resilience: The Key to Overcoming Leadership Challenges   56
   Empathy: The Leadership Superpower   60

The Synergy Between Vision, Resilience, and Empathy	65
Call to Action	66

4. PSYCHOLOGICAL SAFETY — 67
Creating a Culture of Openness and Innovation

Psychological Safety: The Foundation of High-Performing Teams	68
Encouraging Healthy Risk-Taking and Honest Communication	73
Overcoming Resistance to Open Dialogue	76
Call to Action	79

5. BUILDING HIGH — 81
Trust Teams in a Distrustful World

How Leaders Unintentionally Erode Trust—and How to Fix It	82
Common Misconceptions About Trust	84
Creating a Culture of Accountability Without Fear: Redefining Accountability	86
Strategies for Sustaining Trust Over Time	90
Call to Action	95

Part II
NAVIGATING CHANGE WITH AGILITY AND CLARITY

6. LEADING WITHOUT A SCRIPT — 99
Decision-Making in Uncertain Times

Why Rigid Leadership Fails in Fast-Changing Environments	100
Making Confident Decisions Under Pressure	104
Balancing Intuition and Data in Leadership	106
Call to Action	111

7. ADAPTIVE COMMUNICATION — 113
Leading Through Clarity and Connection

Adaptive Communication: Flexing for People and Situations	114
The Role of Transparency and Storytelling in Leadership	118

Digital vs In-Person Leadership in a Hybrid World … 123
Call to Action … 127

8. THE ART OF MANAGING UP, DOWN, AND ACROSS … 129
   Managing Up: Influencing Senior Leaders Without Overstepping … 130
   Managing Across: Leading Lateral Teams and Cross-Functional Groups … 133
   Managing Down: Leading With Empathy, Clarity, and Accountability … 135
   Navigating Power Dynamics and Organizational Politics … 138
   Call to Action … 141

9. LEADING THROUGH CRISIS … 143
   Staying Steady in the Storm
   The Psychology of Crisis Leadership … 144
   Communicating Effectively in High-Pressure Situations: Clarity Over Perfection … 147
   Turning Crises Into Opportunities for Transformation … 151
   Call to Action … 155

Part III
THE FUTURE OF LEADERSHIP AND YOUR LASTING IMPACT

10. THE FUTURE OF LEADERSHIP … 159
    AI, Automation, and the Human Factor
    How Technology Is Reshaping Leadership Roles … 160
    The Enduring Value of Emotional Intelligence and Human Judgment … 163
    Ethical Considerations in AI-Driven Workplaces … 166
    Call to Action … 170

11. THE RESILIENT LEADER
Mastering Growth Through Setbacks — 173

How Failure Shapes Strong Leadership — 173
Learning From Mistakes Without Damaging Credibility — 177
Practical Tools for Personal and Professional Resilience — 181
Call to Action — 185

12. THE LEGACY MINDSET
Investing in People, Not Just Results — 187

Culture Over Outcomes: The Core of a Legacy Mindset — 188
Mentorship: The Multiplier Effect of Great Leadership — 190
Shaping a Leadership Legacy: Intentional Strategies — 193
Call to Action — 196

13. REFLECTION AS A LEADERSHIP TOOL — 197
The Power of Continuous Growth

Self-Awareness: The Hidden Driver of Effective Leadership — 199
Reflective Decision-Making: Slowing Down to Move Faster — 202
Practicing Reflection: Simple, Sustainable Habits for Leaders — 205
Call to Action — 209

14. BRINGING IT ALL TOGETHER — 211
Your Roadmap to Impactful Leadership

The Leadership Shift: A Final Synthesis of Key Lessons — 212
Creating a Personalized Action Plan for Leadership Growth — 215
Becoming a Leader Who Thrives Beyond Authority — 219
Call to Action — 223

Conclusion	225
Glossary	231
References	235
About the Author	243

INTRODUCTION

In a recent workplace survey, 82% of employees said poor leadership makes them feel disengaged, and many consider quitting their jobs because of it (Pappas, 2025). That number is not just concerning, it ought to be a wake-up call.

Leadership was about titles. However, those days are long gone. Currently, leadership is synonymous with trust, influence, adaptability, and above all, human connection.

Let me tell you a quick story.

A few years ago, during a crisis at a major logistics firm, systems shut down nationwide due to a cyberattack. The company's top executives were unreachable, caught in transit without secure communication lines. While chaos rippled through the company, it wasn't a high-ranking executive who stepped up. It was a mid-level team lead—no formal authority, no executive badge, no "chief" in their title—who calmly coordinated regional managers, mobilized local teams, and kept essential deliveries moving. By the time the leaders reestablished contact, the company was already regaining control of the situation.

Such moments not just save the business, they redefine leadership for everyone who witnesses it.

Beyond Authority: Managing Teams in a Rapidly Changing World is a book for people just like that leader—people like you.

This book is for those who find themselves wanting to lead but don't have the title to match. It is for those navigating uncertainty, high stress, resistance, or even outright chaos. It is for aspiring leaders, project managers, team leads, and changemakers who aren't waiting to be given authority but are ready to build influence and make an impact right now.

If you picked up this book, chances are you're facing at least one of the following:

- **You're expected to lead without a formal title.** Maybe you're managing a cross-functional team, driving a key initiative, or trying to influence company culture, but your ideas aren't landing, and your team isn't aligned.
- **You're overwhelmed by how fast everything is changing.** Whether it's technological disruption, industry shakeups, or shifting workplace dynamics, you feel like the rules keep changing, and no one gave you the new playbook.
- **You're struggling to build engagement and trust.** Your team might be resistant, burned out, or just not connecting. You want to foster psychological safety and spark real motivation, but you're unsure how to do this.

- **You find workplace dynamics frustrating or confusing.** Maybe you don't know how to "manage up," or you're tired of politics getting in the way of progress. You want to collaborate better, but you also want to be heard.
- **You're under pressure and doubting yourself.** Leading in high-stress moments can be paralyzing. You're afraid of making the wrong call, or worse, losing credibility.
- **You're not sure how to future-proof your leadership.** With AI, hybrid work, and digital transformation changing everything, you want to stay relevant, but you're unsure which leadership skills you must focus on.

This book is here to help you with all of the above.

WHY THIS BOOK, AND WHY NOW?

Traditional leadership books often start with a top-down model—assuming the reader is a CEO or VP with sweeping authority. But let's face it—the world doesn't work that way anymore.

In workplaces today, leadership is less about control and more about connection. Agility counts more than authority. It's not about commanding from the top—it's about influencing across every level, especially when titles don't guarantee action or respect.

In a time when remote teams, AI disruption, hybrid work culture, and constant volatility are the norm, leaders have no choice but to be more flexible, empathetic, and strategically aware than ever before. You can't just follow a static leadership formula—you need real-time strategies that evolve with the moment.

Beyond Authority is your field guide to the kind of leadership that the world needs. In the following pages, you will learn:

- **practical frameworks** for building trust, communicating effectively, and leading with empathy, even in the face of resistance.
- **modern strategies** for navigating uncertainty, crisis, and change, without losing your composure or your team's confidence.
- **tools for influencing up, down, and across** your organization, even when you lack formal authority or experience in company politics.
- **real-life stories** of leaders who've thrived without titles, adapted during chaos, and redefined what it means to lead in the 21st century.
- **forward-thinking insights** on how AI, automation, and digital transformation are reshaping leadership, and how you can stay ahead of the curve.

Bid rigid, outdated leadership models goodbye. Instead, here, you can embrace honest, human-centered strategies for the messy, unpredictable world we live and work in. You can stop worrying about being "the boss." Instead, you can be someone your team trusts, listens to, and wants to follow, no matter what your role on paper says.

WHAT MAKES THIS BOOK DIFFERENT?

A few things set this book apart are that it is:

- **Not for executives alone:** It's for team leads, project managers, middle managers, and rising stars. It's for anyone trying to make a difference without waiting for permission.
- **Rooted in real-world leadership:** Without ivory tower theories, you will discover practical, field-tested strategies for leading in fast-paced, high-stakes, real-time environments.
- **Meant to bridge leadership with agility:** You'll learn how to lead when everything changes, the plan falls apart, or crises demand fast thinking and deep calm.
- **People-first.** Gone are the days when leadership was just about output. Today, it's about culture, safety, and empathy. This book teaches you how to lead with emotional intelligence, build resilient teams, and foster innovation.
- **Created for the future:** While honoring timeless principles, this book equips you for what's next, so you can lead not just today, but for tomorrow's world.

By the end of this book, you will not only feel more prepared to lead, and feel more empowered. You will have the tools, mindset, and strategies to rise to the challenge, even when the ground is shifting beneath your feet.

Leadership is how you show up.

So, let's begin, if you are ready, shall we?

PART I
RETHINKING LEADERSHIP IN A CHANGING WORLD

(WHY TRADITIONAL AUTHORITY NO LONGER WORKS, AND WHAT TO DO INSTEAD.)

THE NEW LEADERSHIP PARADIGM

THRIVING BEYOND AUTHORITY

> *A leader is a dealer in hope.*
>
> — NAPOLEON BONAPARTE

For decades, leadership was defined by authority—clear hierarchies, rigid structures, and top-down commands. The leader gave orders, and others followed. This traditional command-and-control model thrived in a world where stability and predictability were the norm.

However, things have changed. Today's workplaces are fast-paced, digital-first, and increasingly decentralized. Teams are remote, cross-functional, and diverse. Information flows freely, change happens rapidly, and innovation depends on collaboration, not compliance. In this environment, holding a title or sitting at the top of an organizational chart no longer guarantees influence or impact. *What does?*, you may ask. Trust, empathy, adaptability, and the ability to inspire, and not instruct, are today's mantras. Influence is the key, not authority.

The modern leader isn't the loudest voice in the room, but the one others choose to follow. They build cultures where people feel seen, heard, and empowered. They navigate uncertainty with resilience and lead through change with clarity and compassion.

This shift calls for a new leadership paradigm—rooted in relationships, emotional intelligence, and the capacity to grow with and through others. It's not giving orders, but creating alignment, fostering trust, and leading by example.

The future of leadership has already arrived. The question you must ask is, "Am I ready for it?"

THE SHIFT FROM CONTROL-BASED TO INFLUENCE-DRIVEN LEADERSHIP

Traditionally, leaders were viewed as the ultimate authority figures. Their word was final, and their decisions unquestioned. In this top-down model, leadership was exercised through formal power like titles, positions, and hierarchical control. The corporate world was structured like a pyramid —each layer reporting to the one above it, with power concentrated at the top.

In such systems, compliance was the currency of success. Employees followed instructions not because they believed in them, but because they feared the consequences of disobedience. Motivation was extrinsic. They were driven by rewards, punishments, and job security. Though this may have garnered obedience, creativity in such environments was often stifled. This is because innovation rarely thrives in environments where risk-taking is punished and dissent is discouraged.

This control-based approach had an age and market. It worked in stable, industrial-era workplaces, where processes were predictable and tasks were routine. But today's world is anything but predictable.

Why the Old Model no Longer Works

In the 21st-century workplace, the flaws of traditional leadership are increasingly exposed. Several powerful shifts have rendered the old model obsolete.

- **The rise of knowledge work**: Modern organizations rely on "knowledge workers"—people whose primary contribution is intellectual, not physical. These individuals often possess expertise that surpasses that of their leaders. A software engineer, for example, may know far more about coding than their manager. In such scenarios, leadership based solely on authority breaks down. Collaboration, mutual respect, and shared decision-making become essential.
- **The digital transformation:** Remote and hybrid work models have reshaped how teams function. With employees scattered across cities, countries, and time zones, micromanagement is not just impractical, it's counterproductive. Workers now crave autonomy and flexibility, and successful leaders are those who empower rather than control.

Command-and-control tactics erode trust, reduce morale, and lead to disengagement.
- **The speed of change:** Technological advancements are accelerating at an unprecedented pace. New tools, platforms, and business models emerge constantly, demanding rapid adaptation. Hierarchical organizations, with their layers of approval and bureaucracy, struggle to keep up. Innovation depends on agility, and agility requires decentralization—giving teams the freedom to act and make decisions quickly.
- **Generational shifts:** The workforce is increasingly dominated by Millennials and Gen Z—generations that value purpose, inclusion, and empowerment. These employees are not content with following orders; they want to contribute meaningfully, understand the "why" behind decisions, and be part of something bigger than themselves. A leadership style rooted in control and hierarchy simply doesn't resonate with them.

In this new reality, leadership must evolve to include at its fore, influence. Influence-driven leadership is based on credibility, empathy, and trust. It's earning the right to lead, not assuming it by default.

What Influence-Driven Leadership Looks Like

Influential leaders focus on inspiring others. They mentor, coach, and facilitate rather than dictate. They ask questions, listen deeply, and create environments where people feel safe to speak up and take risks. They don't lead through fear; they lead through vision, values, and vulnerability.

There is a tendency to conflate influence-driven leadership with passivity or indecision. But make no mistake, influential leadership is also being adaptive—knowing when to step in and when to step back, or when to push and when to support. It requires emotional intelligence, self-awareness, and the humility to recognize that leadership is a relationship, not a position.

A Study in Difference

To understand the contrast between control-based and influence-driven leadership, consider two high-profile tech leaders—Elon Musk and Satya Nadella.

Musk is well-known for his bold vision and relentless drive. At companies like Tesla and X (previously Twitter), he has demonstrated a high-pressure, command-heavy leadership style. He makes rapid decisions, sets aggressive goals, and demands high performance. Though his approach has led to breakthroughs, it has also led to burnout, higher turnover of staff, and public scrutiny (Taplin, 2024).

In contrast, Satya Nadella's leadership at Microsoft (Meier, 2024) has been a masterclass in influence. When he took over as CEO in 2014, the company was struggling with internal silos and stagnation. Nadella focused on empathy, inclusion, and a growth mindset. He reshaped Microsoft's culture, encouraging collaboration and curiosity. Under his leadership, the company revived its innovation engine and saw record financial performance and employee engagement.

Our aim here is not to criticize, but to learn. Neither of the leaders above is wholly right or wrong—context matters. Musk's style works in high-risk, high-reward environments where speed trumps stability. Nadella's approach thrives in complex, knowledge-based organizations that require cross-functional synergy. The key takeaway is that modern leadership is not a single entity. It demands flexibility, not dogma.

The shift from control to influence marks a fundamental evolution in how we understand leadership. Authority may get people to comply, but influence gets them to commit. And in today's volatile, uncertain, and interconnected world, commitment is far more valuable than compliance.

Great leaders no longer seek to be feared; instead, they seek to be trusted. They no longer need to demand loyalty because they earn it. They don't impose their vision, but co-create it with their teams. As the workplace continues to evolve, the leaders who thrive will understand that real power doesn't come from control; it comes from connection.

WHY ADAPTABILITY MATTERS MORE THAN RIGID POWER

In a world where disruption is the new normal, the most valuable leadership trait isn't authority—it's adaptability. The leaders who succeed today aren't the ones who cling to power or resist change, but those who can shift gears, reframe problems, and respond to new realities with clarity and confidence.

The Leadership Mindset Shift: From Fixed to Fluid

For much of the 20th century, leadership operated on a simple assumption—the future was predictable. Leaders crafted five-year plans, set long-term goals, and built systems designed for control and consistency. The mindset was fixed, and leaders were expected to stick to the plan and maintain order. This approach made sense in stable, immutable markets, where the only change was incremental and competition was localized.

But the 21st century is anything but stable. Technology evolves faster than strategy. Market shifts can happen overnight. A single social media trend, global event, or algorithm update can flip an entire industry. In this dynamic environment, rigid leadership becomes a liability. Leaders who insist on sticking to old plans, enforcing outdated policies, or maintaining tight control often end up slowing their teams down, or worse, leading them into irrelevance.

The world demands a fluid leadership mindset. Instead of clinging to certainty, modern successful leaders embrace ambiguity. They must be comfortable making decisions without having all the answers and be willing to pivot when the facts change. The ability to adapt isn't just useful, it's essential.

Key Traits of an Adaptive Leader

Adaptability in leadership doesn't have to be improvising aimlessly. It's developing specific traits that allow a leader to stay grounded while still moving with the times.

- **Openness to change:** Adaptive leaders are curious by nature. They don't resist change, but anticipate it. They're willing to unlearn what no longer works and explore new approaches, even when those approaches feel uncomfortable at first. This openness allows them to lead innovation rather than react to it. They ask, "What if there's a better way?" instead of saying, "This is how we've always done it."
- **Emotional intelligence:** In times of change, people look to leaders for emotional cues. Adaptive leaders know how to read the room. They understand the fears, hopes, and motivations of their team members. Rather than applying a single, unvaried approach, they adjust their style to fit the needs of the moment. They stay calm under pressure, communicate with empathy, and create psychological safety, so others feel confident maneuvering uncertainty too.
- **Situational awareness:** Rigid leaders follow the same script regardless of the context. Adaptive leaders, by contrast, are highly attuned to their surroundings. They know when to lead from the front, step back and listen, and delegate authority to those better equipped to handle specific challenges. Instead of seeing leadership as control, they see it as orchestration.
- **Empowered decision-making:** In fast-paced environments, hesitation can be costly. Adaptive leaders are decisive, but their decisions are informed by a mix of data, insight, and intuition. Though unafraid to make bold moves, they also know when to turn around and change their tactics. They empower their teams to act without waiting for

permission in certain situations, creating a culture where initiative is rewarded, and red tape is minimized.
- **Resilience under pressure:** Avoiding setbacks is not adaptability. Bouncing back from setbacks, or resilience, is at the heart of adaptive thinking. Adaptive leaders view failure as feedback, and not necessarily as defeat. They model resilience, demonstrating their ability to recover, regroup, and refocus. Even in a crisis, they remain forward-thinking and solution-oriented.

A Study in Adaptability

In the early 2000s, Netflix was known for its DVD-by-mail rental service, which was a disruptive model at the time. However, CEO Reed Hastings saw a bigger shift coming—the rise of streaming technology. Many leaders in his position might have stuck to the successful DVD model, reluctant to jeopardize a proven business.

Instead, Hastings made a bold move. He led Netflix's transition from physical rentals to digital streaming, way before it became the industry norm. And he didn't stop there. Recognizing that content, not just distribution, would define the future of entertainment, he invested heavily in original series, starting with "House of Cards" (2013) and eventually building a global content empire.

This adaptability positioned Netflix as a leader in the streaming revolution. Meanwhile, companies that clung to old models, like Blockbuster, were left behind (Nakanishi, 2025).

So, what is the lesson here? Success in one era doesn't guarantee relevance in the next. Adaptive leadership is about survival and seizing the future before others see it coming.

The Adaptive Advantage

In today's volatile and fast-changing world, leadership can no longer rely on rigid power structures, long-term predictability, or hierarchical control. The strongest leaders are not those who hold the tightest grip, but those who can bend without breaking, those who can read the moment, rally their teams, and respond with agility.

Adaptability is a strategic advantage. As industries evolve, technologies shift, and expectations rise, the ability to adapt becomes the defining quality of successful leaders.

Now, ask yourself, "Are you holding on to a leadership model built for a world that no longer exists? Or are you ready to lead with agility, empathy, and vision into the future?"

The choice, as well as the challenge, is yours!

THE CURIOUS CASE OF LEADERS WHO THRIVE WITHOUT AUTHORITY: SOME CASE STUDIES

In an era where influence often trumps authority, some of the most effective leaders in the world have demonstrated that real leadership is centered around trust, empathy, vision, and connection.

Let us explore three remarkable case studies of leaders who redefined leadership by thriving without relying solely on formal authority.

Case 1: Indra Nooyi—Leading With Influence, Not Fear

When Indra Nooyi took the reins as CEO of PepsiCo, she did more than just manage a global beverage empire; she transformed its leadership culture. Rather than ruling with an iron fist, Nooyi led with empathy, emotional intelligence, and strategic vision.

Her leadership philosophy centered around "Performance with Purpose," was a commitment to aligning profit with social responsibility (Ignatius, 2021). She believed that long-term success came not from strong numbers, but strong values. Her approach inspired deep employee loyalty and consumer trust.

Nooyi frequently reached out to the families of her executive team, writing personal letters to express appreciation for their support. This seemingly small gesture created massive goodwill, reinforcing her belief that leadership is deeply human.

Key lesson: Influence-driven leadership—when rooted in empathy and purpose—generates loyalty, engagement, and sustainable success far more effectively than fear-based authority ever could.

Case 2: Nelson Mandela—Leading Without Formal Power

Before he became South Africa's first Black president, Nelson Mandela was a prisoner, stripped of all political authority, and yet one of the most powerful voices in the country.

From a jail cell on Robben Island, Mandela inspired a global movement. His vision of unity, his unwavering moral compass, and his refusal to retaliate created a foundation for healing in a country fractured by apartheid. Even without a position of official leadership, he shaped history through influence, conviction, and moral courage.

Mandela realized leadership is not control, but shaping perspectives and building bridges. When he finally assumed formal power, he governed with humility, forgiveness, and a focus on reconciliation rather than revenge (Munn, 2013).

Key lesson: True leadership is about inspiring people toward a shared vision, even when you have no official power. Influence trumps even institution.

Case 3: Jacinda Ardern—Leading Through Empathy and Adaptability

As the Prime Minister of New Zealand, Jacinda Ardern led her country through some of the most challenging times in its modern history, including the Christchurch mosque attacks and the COVID-19 pandemic (Christman, n.d.). Far from brute force or political posturing, she led with empathy, clarity, and emotional intelligence.

Her response to the Christchurch tragedy was swift, compassionate, and inclusive. She stood shoulder-to-shoulder with the Muslim community, donning a hijab and speaking words of comfort that resonated far beyond politics. During the pandemic, her clear and calm communication, paired with decisive action, made New Zealand a global model for effective crisis leadership.

Ardern proved that soft skills are hard power when used right. She didn't have to command obedience, she earned trust, and with it, the willingness of citizens to follow.

Key lesson: Empathy isn't a weakness—it's a superpower, especially in high-stakes, high-emotion situations.

Now that we have looked at a lot of theory on leadership strategies, how can we turn this knowledge into practical, actionable steps?

APPLYING THE NEW LEADERSHIP PARADIGM

The leaders, whose examples we discussed above, didn't rely on rigid structures or formal control. They succeeded by leading through influence, connecting with people, inspiring belief, and building trust. So, how can *you* adopt this influence-driven model of leadership?

Shifting From Authority to Influence: A Personal Leadership Exercise

1. **Reflection:** Think of a time when you or someone you observed led successfully without relying on title

or authority. What qualities were most used—empathy, communication, storytelling, trust, or…?
2. **Assessment:** Where in your current leadership approach are you relying too heavily on control? Where can you instead cultivate influence by building relationships and empowering others?
3. **Action plan:** Use the following whenever in doubt and if contextually appropriate:
   - Listen more than you speak. People feel valued when they're heard.
   - Seek to understand before giving orders. Ask questions and gather all the input you possibly can.
   - Empower others to take ownership to create space for autonomy and creativity.
   - Communicate your vision clearly and consistently, because a shared vision provides direction and meaning, and fuels commitment.

Now, let us also briefly touch upon some practical tools for you.

Practical Tools for Influence-Driven Leadership

Adopting an influence-first mindset doesn't necessitate leaving structure behind. You can use smarter tools that foster connection and trust.

1. **The trust equation:** Trust = (Credibility X Reliability X Intimacy) / Self-Orientation. This model, popularized by Charles Green (*The Trust Equation*, 2019), reminds us that trust comes from competence,

consistency, personal connection, and low personal ego. Some important terms to remember here are:
   - **Credibility:** The believability of your words, reflecting your expertise and honesty.
   - **Reliability:** The consistency of your actions, demonstrating dependability and follow-through.
   - **Intimacy:** The safety others feel in sharing with you, built through empathy and discretion.
   - **Self-orientation:** The degree to which your focus is on others versus yourself; lower self-orientation enhances trust.
2. **Storytelling for influence:** Facts inform, but stories inspire. Influence-driven leaders use narrative to make abstract goals personal and relatable. Share real stories of impact, growth, and purpose with your team often.
3. **The power of questions:** If commanding is telling people what to do, questioning invites engagement and ownership. Replace "Here's what I want" with "What do you think would work best?" It sparks dialogue, not defiance.

Modern leadership demands more than a seat at the head of the table. It requires one to connect with people, earn their trust, and guide them through complexity with clarity and empathy. The leaders who thrive are those who listen, empower, and evolve. They don't just hold positions, but create movements, spark innovation, and cultivate loyalty. The key takeaway is that leadership is much greater than a title. It is making a positive impact.

CALL TO ACTION

- Take a moment to reflect on your leadership style. Are you relying too much on authority? Are there moments when you could lead through influence instead?
- Consider one simple shift you can make today. Maybe it's listening more intentionally. Maybe it's asking a powerful question instead of giving a directive. Maybe it's trusting someone on your team to take the lead.

In whatever change you can make, feel free to start small, but start now.

In this new era of leadership, your real power comes from the difference you can make.

LEADING WITH INFLUENCE

THE ART OF TRUST AND CREDIBILITY

> *Your words and deeds must match if you expect employees to trust in your leadership.*
>
> — KEVIN KRUSE

True leadership inspires action, and not obligation. While authority may secure short-term obedience, it rarely cultivates any lasting impact. Influence, on the other hand, nurtures trust, loyalty, and a shared sense of purpose that outlives any positional power.

Consider two managers in the same organization. One operates by the book, using their title as a hammer, demanding results, enforcing rules, and expecting obedience. Their team complies, but morale is low, and staff attrition is high. The second manager leads with empathy and integrity. They listen more than they lecture, invest in their people, and model the behavior they want to see. Their team is not only productive but also fiercely loyal and willing to go the extra mile—not because they have to, but because they want to.

In time, the first manager may see results falter as disengagement spreads. The second manager, meanwhile, builds a resilient culture rooted in mutual respect. In the latter case, influence, not fear, becomes the driver of performance.

This chapter explores why authority alone is a fragile form of leadership, and how building influence leads to sustainable success. We'll dissect what makes influence so powerful and how to develop it in ways that inspire, empower, and endure.

AUTHORITY VS TRUE LEADERSHIP: UNDERSTANDING THE DIFFERENCE

In every workplace, leadership appears in different forms. Some leaders operate through formal authority, or power from a title or organizational hierarchy. Others lead through influence, or power from character, vision, and the ability to connect with others. While both approaches can drive action and performance, the outcomes they produce differ significantly.

Authority-Based Leadership in Practice

As we have already seen, authority-based leadership relies on a leader's position within a system. It's the kind of leadership that stems from a job title, rank, or organizational chart. This structure creates an obligation to follow, and employees respond because of the leader's status rather than their example or insight.

Leaders who depend heavily on authority often exhibit similar behaviors. They tend to micromanage tasks, holding a tight grip on decision-making. Rather than encouraging independence, they seek control. Instead of inspiring a sense of ownership, they focus on enforcing rules and maintaining hierarchy. These leaders may treat feedback as a threat and discourage open discussion, stifling creativity and limiting team engagement.

The result is a workplace where compliance matters more than contribution. Performance may appear steady, but beneath the surface, motivation declines, innovation stalls, and trust erodes. Over time, authority-driven environments become fragile and vulnerable to burnout and stagnation.

Influence-Based Leadership in Practice

Influence-based leadership grows from trust and earned respect. It emerges when a leader consistently models integrity, competence, and empathy. This form of leadership doesn't require a title to hold weight. People follow because they believe in the leader's message and values. They commit to the vision, not because they're ordered to, but because they see its purpose and want to be part of it.

Influential leaders create space for others to grow. They delegate responsibility with confidence, offer support without smothering, and focus on outcomes over control. Their communication is transparent and inclusive. They ask questions, invite feedback, and treat disagreement as a doorway to new perspectives. This openness builds a culture of psychological safety, where people feel seen, heard, and valued.

Through influence, leaders mobilize teams around shared goals. They bring out the best in others by helping them discover meaning in their work. Instead of pushing people with pressure, they pull them forward with purpose.

A Tale of Two Leaders

Few leaders illustrate the difference between authority and influence more clearly than Steve Jobs. In the early years of Apple, right after he co-founded it in 1976, he was widely known for his intense personality, and autocratic and demanding style. Driven by perfectionism and control, he often clashed with team members. His brilliance was unquestioned, but his leadership alienated colleagues and strained relationships. Eventually, the board had very little choice but to oust him from the company in 1985.

Years later, Jobs returned to a then-nearly bankrupt Apple in 1997, with a very different approach. His creative drive remained, but his leadership style had matured. He focused less on control and more on cultivating an environment where talent could thrive. He hired exceptional people and trusted them to innovate. His ability to inspire became his greatest asset. By aligning the company around a bold vision and fostering a culture of excellence, Jobs transformed Apple into one of the most influential brands in the world.

This evolution demonstrates a powerful lesson. Command alone can drive short-term gains, but it often burns bridges. Influence, on the other hand, brings people together, sustains momentum, and leaves a deeper mark (Loonam, 2024).

The Lasting Impact of Influence

When authority is the only tool in a leader's kit, trust remains shallow. People may concede, but few will truly commit. In contrast, leaders who focus on influence build resilient teams—ones that adapt, grow, and perform well under pressure. Curiosity sparks innovation. They attract loyalty by making people feel valued.

Influence-based leadership doesn't require charisma or fame. It starts with listening, caring, and leading by example. It grows with consistency, humility, and a willingness to learn. While titles may change and structures shift, influence always remains. It travels with the leader and leaves a legacy that far outlasts formal authority.

In the sections ahead, we'll explore how influence can be developed and applied in everyday leadership. Through practical strategies and real-world stories, you can see how trust, empathy, and vision shape the kind of leadership that truly makes a difference.

BUILDING TRUST: THE FOUNDATION OF LEADERSHIP INFLUENCE

Influence gains strength when anchored in trust. It is the silent agreement between the leader and their team, building a space for risk-taking, creativity, and meaningful collaboration. Trust begets belief in a shared direction, even when the path forward feels uncertain. Without it, even the most skilled leaders struggle to inspire true commitment.

Teams thrive when they know their leader has their back. When trust is present, people speak freely, contribute fully, and support each other through challenges. Decisions carry weight because they come from someone whose words match their actions. In such an environment, leadership becomes a partnership rather than a directive.

Trust is more than a personality trait. It's a deliberate practice. It must be earned, protected, and continuously nurtured. At its core, trust rests on three foundational pillars: transparency, competence, and authenticity.

Transparency: Creating Openness and Psychological Safety

Transparency signals respect. When leaders communicate openly, they invite others into the process. Sharing information, especially during difficult moments, fosters a sense of inclusion. It reassures teams that leadership operates with integrity and values their understanding.

Transparent leaders speak with clarity. They update their teams regularly and provide context, even when the circumstances are complex. Rather than shielding people from hard truths, they share them constructively, creating trust through honesty.

Admitting errors is a powerful act. Leaders who own their mistakes show humility and courage. This behavior normalizes learning, softens the fear of failure, and strengthens the team's bond. Teams become more willing to take initiative, ask questions, and offer bold ideas, secure in the knowledge that their leader will meet them with support, not shame.

Creating a culture of transparency also means encouraging dialogue. Leaders who ask for input—and genuinely consider it—nurture psychological safety. People speak up because they know their voices carry weight. This flow of honest conversation becomes the lifeblood of innovation.

For example, Sid Sijbrandij, CEO and Co-founder of GitLab, promotes radical transparency. When the company faced a serious cyber incident in early 2017 that disrupted operations, they didn't handle it behind closed doors. Instead, the entire recovery process was live-streamed on YouTube for the world to see. This wasn't a PR stunt. It reflected a deep-rooted cultural commitment to openness. GitLab maintains a publicly accessible employee handbook, conducts most internal conversations in open channels, and even shares the personal preferences of its CEO, like his typical travel setup: aisle seats, extra legroom on international flights, and check-in luggage only if the trip lasts more than a day (Macpherson, 2021).

Competence: Gaining Trust Through Expertise and Consistency

Competence forms the practical core of trust. People place their confidence in leaders who consistently deliver. Far from technical skill alone, it's about sound judgment, informed action, and a steady hand when challenges arise.

A competent leader seeks knowledge continuously. They read, listen, ask questions, and surround themselves with diverse expertise. Their curiosity keeps them sharp, and their decisions reflect a thoughtful blend of data, experience, and intuition.

Delivering results builds trust, but doing so consistently solidifies it. When leaders follow through on commitments, their credibility deepens. They become reliable touchstones in a world that often changes quickly.

Competence also means knowing when to pause. Leaders earn respect by considering multiple viewpoints before making decisions. This balance of confidence and care reassures teams and reinforces stability.

Germany's former Chancellor Angela Merkel earned international admiration for her calm, competent leadership during major global crises. Her background in science and her data-driven approach allowed her to communicate complex issues with clarity. Merkel always avoided pompous or emotional oratory. Instead, she focused on facts, measured responses, and steady progress. Her consistent, informed leadership earned her the long-term trust of both her nation and the wider world, especially during the Eurozone crisis and the refugee crisis (Esch, 2021).

Authenticity: Leading With Integrity and Relatability

Authenticity is the human side of trust. People are drawn to leaders who are real, lead with their heart, speak with sincerity, and remain grounded in their values. Authenticity removes the mask of perfection and replaces it with genuine presence.

An authentic leader expresses emotion in ways that resonate. They show passion for their mission, compassion for their people, and courage in vulnerable moments. Rather than presenting a polished façade, they reveal the person behind the title.

Genuine interactions build emotional connection. When leaders speak plainly, listen attentively, and act without pretense, others respond with openness. This type of leadership removes barriers and invites collaboration rooted in mutual respect.

Living by values is the strongest signal of authenticity. Whether facing pressure, success, or criticism, authentic leaders stay anchored in their beliefs. Their choices reflect their principles, and their integrity remains intact, even when the easier route might lead elsewhere.

Throughout her career, Oprah Winfrey has led by being unapologetically herself. She speaks from personal experience, connects deeply with others, and holds space for meaningful conversation. Her leadership style, both on and off-screen, reflects empathy, truth-telling, and unrelenting commitment to her mission. Audiences and collaborators trust her because she leads with authenticity. Her influence extends far beyond media, shaping philanthropic efforts, social dialogue, and leadership philosophy across industries (George, 2024).

Trust in Action

Together, transparency, competence, and authenticity form the foundation for trust in leadership. Each pillar supports a different dimension of influence—clarity, capability, and connection. When leaders embody these traits, trust becomes more than a feeling; it becomes a force.

Teams led by trust-driven leaders tend to achieve more, stay longer together, and grow stronger. They operate with shared purpose and take ownership of their work. In such cases, leadership is not control but enabling people to do their best work—and to believe in why it matters.

Building trust requires attention, humility, and time. It asks leaders to show up consistently, lead with intention, and prioritize people over position. Those who rise to this challenge gain more than performance. They gain enduring influence that shapes culture, inspires loyalty, and drives real progress.

We have looked at some theory related to influence. Now, let us look at it in practice. What can you, as a leader, do to inspire trust and credibility?

INFLUENCE TECHNIQUES FOR EFFECTIVE LEADERSHIP

Influence empowers leaders to inspire action, strengthen collaboration, and guide others toward shared success. Far from manipulation, influence is an ethical practice rooted in psychology, empathy, and purpose. It builds momentum through trust and connection, not pressure or control.

Understanding the science of influence offers valuable insight into human behavior. Research reveals consistent patterns in how people make decisions, form loyalties, and align with a cause (Hornsby & Love, 2020). These patterns form the basis of influence, and when used responsibly, they elevate leadership from routine direction to transformational impact.

The Science of Influence: How People Are Persuaded

People respond to fairness, connection, and shared belief (Zainuddin & Isa, 2019; Bettencourt & Brown, 1997). These psychological principles serve as powerful levers for influence:

- **Reciprocity:** When leaders act generously and treat others with fairness, people respond with trust and commitment. A spirit of giving often leads to a culture of loyalty.
- **Social proof:** Individuals look to the actions of others when forming decisions. When a group believes in a leader's vision, it reinforces confidence and spreads alignment organically.
- **Authority (credibility-based):** Influence grows stronger when a leader demonstrates expertise. People respect those who consistently show skill, insight, and informed decision-making.
- **Liking:** People are more receptive to those they feel connected to. Respect, relatability, and kindness foster a bond that enhances influence.

When integrated into leadership practice, the above characteristics allow a leader's message to resonate deeply and authentically.

Five Proven Influence Strategies for Leaders

Building influence is both an art and a strategy. The following techniques harness behavioral insights to create meaningful leadership moments and lasting results.

1. **Lead by example (modeling behavior):** Leaders who live their values set a standard that others want to follow. Modeling integrity, resilience, and collaboration signals what matters most. This is not through directives, but through action.

When Howard Schultz returned to lead Starbucks during the global recession in 2008, he didn't stick to conservative policies. To navigate the crisis, multiple employees were let go, and numerous store locations closed down. But Schultz also oversaw the acquisition of several beverage companies in both the U.S. and China, introduced a customer rewards program, and implemented ethical sourcing practices. His bold expansion into China was especially impressive, successfully entering a market traditionally centered around tea-drinking rather than coffee (*Howard Schultz leadership style*, 2023).

Modeling behavior is a daily opportunity. Every choice, reaction, and gesture sends a message. When leaders show up consistently in alignment with their vision, they become living proof of the values they advocate.

2. **Tell powerful stories (storytelling for influence):** Storytelling connects information to emotion. While data supports decisions, stories move people to act. A compelling narrative brings purpose to life and makes abstract goals personal. Great leaders craft stories that reflect real challenges and meaningful growth. They use metaphors to illuminate complex ideas and invite listeners to see themselves in the

journey. When you can make the audience the hero of the story, engagement will rise.

Martin Luther King Jr.'s famous "I Have a Dream" speech (King, 1963) endures because of its vivid, hope-filled imagery and inclusive message. His words invited people to imagine a better future, and believe they could help create it.

In a team setting, stories can highlight lessons learned, celebrate progress, or reconnect people to the mission. A well-timed story turns a meeting into a moment of shared purpose.

3. **Ask, don't tell (the power of strategic questions):** Questions invite curiosity. They empower others to think independently and contribute their voice. Rather than pushing people toward an outcome, strategic questions lead them there with ownership and insight.

Thoughtful questions like:

- What do you think is the best approach?
- How does this support our broader vision?
- What's holding us back—and how can we overcome it?

can reframe challenges, surface hidden concerns, and inspire solutions.

This approach echoes the Socratic method (Kraut, 2025), where inquiry sparks discovery. In asking instead of instructing, leaders encourage reflection, unlock deeper understanding, and strengthen team confidence.

4. **Build alliances and leverage networks:** Leadership thrives in connection. Influence expands through relationships built on mutual respect and shared goals. Leaders who engage stakeholders, support their peers, and seek common ground multiply their reach.

Sheryl Sandberg, in her role at Facebook and later, emphasized the importance of strong, diverse networks (Adams, 2013). Her ability to connect across teams, industries, and initiatives allowed her to shape decisions and champion big ideas with broad support.

Building alliances begins with contribution. Leaders who offer support without conditions earn trust and open doors. As relationships deepen, influence flows more freely, reaching across teams, departments, and communities.

5. **Master the art of presence and active listening:** Presence creates impact without needing volume. A leader's calm, confident energy in a room can carry more weight than a dozen directives. True presence means being fully engaged in the moment—listening, observing, and responding with intention.

Barack Obama's leadership style (McPheat, 2024) is reflected in his speeches and interactions. He paused at key moments, allowed ideas to settle, and responded clearly. His listening style gave people the sense that their voice mattered, and that leadership was a shared space, not a distant force.

You can cultivate presence by:

- maintaining eye contact with calm confidence
- letting silence work—pausing can highlight important points
- listening without planning your next response

These behaviors transform ordinary conversations into moments of influence.

Effective leaders influence with purpose, guided by empathy and supported by strategy. Leaders foster real change by understanding how people are persuaded, and using techniques rooted in integrity. Influence turns ideas into action, unites individuals into teams, and brings vision to life.

OVERCOMING COMMON INFLUENCE BARRIERS

Even the most well-intentioned leaders can struggle with influence when certain key elements are missing. Influence isn't automatic, but grows from consistent effort, clarity of purpose, and authentic relationships. When those foundations weaken, so does a leader's ability to inspire meaningful action. Understanding what creates these gaps is the first step toward rebuilding a strong and lasting influence.

Why Some Leaders Struggle to Influence Effectively

Influence depends on trust and credibility. When people question a leader's expertise or judgment, they hesitate to follow. Confidence in leadership comes from a track record of sound decisions, thoughtful communication, and reliability under pressure.

Inconsistencies in behavior can also dilute influence. When a leader's actions shift unpredictably or stray from their stated values, it creates confusion. People rely on consistency to feel secure in their environment. When leadership wavers, commitment weakens.

Another challenge arises when leaders focus too heavily on securing immediate results through authority. While direct control may generate quick responses, it rarely builds loyalty. Influence, in contrast, gains power over time as people align with a shared vision, feel respected, and see their role in the bigger picture.

How to Fix Influence Gaps

Strengthening influence begins with self-awareness. Leaders must take time to assess how they're perceived, not through assumptions, but by seeking feedback. This feedback might come through formal assessments, candid conversations, or anonymous surveys. Asking thoughtful questions like, "Where do I add the most value?" or "What could I do differently to strengthen our collaboration?" opens doors to insight and improvement.

Consistency enhances credibility. Aligning words with actions signals integrity. When a leader follows through on commitments—whether in project timelines or cultural values—they show reliability. Small positive actions, repeated regularly, reinforce a leader's message and build a stable platform for influence.

Transparency deepens trust. When decisions are explained with clarity and context, people understand the rationale behind them. This creates buy-in, even during challenging moments. Leaders who share the "why" behind their choices offer others a sense of inclusion and respect, strengthening alignment and loyalty.

Relationships remain at the core of lasting influence. Influence grows stronger in environments where trust, understanding, and shared goals are nurtured. Investing in genuine connections means taking time to know team members, understand their motivations, and support their growth. This foundation encourages mutual support, open communication, and a shared commitment to success.

Leaders who cultivate these habits find that influence begins to flow more naturally. Instead of needing to urge or control, their presence invites engagement. Their ideas resonate because they come from someone trusted, consistent, and connected.

In today's evolving world, influence driven by trust and credibility has become the defining mark of effective leadership. Leaders who build trust, lead with purpose, and inspire others, create a lasting impact.

CALL TO ACTION

- Take a moment to reflect: What's one action you can take today to strengthen your influence—being more trustworthy, more consistent, or more authentic in your leadership?

Start here, and let the result ripple outward.

VISION, RESILIENCE, AND EMPATHY

THE CORE LEADERSHIP TRIO

> *Leadership is the capacity to translate vision into reality.*
>
> — WARREN G. BENNIS

In today's dynamic and unpredictable world, leadership demands more than titles and tactical plans, it calls for a deeper foundation rooted in character and clarity. At the heart of truly impactful leadership lie three essential qualities—vision, resilience, and empathy. These pillars shape a leader's response to challenges and define the tone and trajectory of their influence.

Imagine two leaders confronted by a sudden crisis. One remains composed, guided by a clear sense of direction, inner strength, and a genuine concern for their team. The other stumbles through reactionary decisions, struggling to keep pace with the events unfolding. As the situation unfolds, you can clearly see the distinction between leading and merely managing.

This chapter explores how vision provides purpose, resilience fuels perseverance, and empathy fosters trust, together creating a leadership approach that endures through disruption and change. Whether you're leading a team, an organization, or your own life, cultivating these three traits will shape your ability to inspire, navigate uncertainty, and leave behind a meaningful legacy.

VISION: LEADING WITH CLARITY IN UNCERTAIN TIMES

In times of uncertainty, vision acts as a compass. It provides direction when familiar markers disappear, helping leaders chart a course through unfamiliar terrain. With rapid technological shifts, economic turbulence, and evolving global expectations, the need for a strong vision has only grown stronger. It is the steady light that guides both individuals and organizations through periods of ambiguity and complexity.

Vision brings meaning to motion. While strategies and KPIs shape how an organization operates daily, vision defines why it exists in the first place. It sets the destination, while giving people something greater than themselves to believe in. When clearly communicated, vision inspires alignment and commitment and momentum, even when conditions are tougher than usual.

VISION, RESILIENCE, AND EMPATHY | 53

Aligning Vision With Core Values and Purpose

Vision becomes truly powerful when **grounded in values**. Vision isn't setting ambitious targets; it is articulating a deeper purpose. Leaders who build their vision on a foundation of shared values are more likely to foster loyalty, trust, and genuine engagement.

When the famous outdoor apparel company, Patagonia, declared its commitment to environmental responsibility (VanderLinden, 2024), it wasn't just a change in branding, it was a reflection of its identity. The company's actions aligned seamlessly with its message, from supply chain transparency to funding grassroots environmental movements. The clarity of that vision resonated with customers and employees alike, cultivating a sense of shared mission.

Leaders who take the time to reflect on what their organizations stand for and why they exist are better equipped to create a vision that transcends profits. If a leader can link business objectives to broader societal or environmental purposes, they turn day-to-day tasks into meaningful contributions to a larger whole.

Making Vision Tangible and Actionable

A compelling vision must do more than just inspire. Ultimately, it must drive action. Abstract ideals, no matter how eloquent, won't spark change unless they are paired with clarity and structure. Great leaders take bold ideas and translate them into concrete steps that people can understand, rally around, and execute.

Breaking down a long-term vision into **short-term, achievable goals** ensures steady progress. When people can see how their efforts contribute to something larger, it increases motivation. Involving teams in shaping this vision further enhances buy-in and ownership. It turns around passive followers into active participants.

Storytelling plays a crucial role in making a vision memorable and sustainable. Narratives stick. They humanize goals, illustrate impact, and make the abstract feel real. When Satya Nadella took the helm at Microsoft, he communicated a clear narrative of transformation (*Satya Nadella's Transformation of Microsoft*, 2024). He emphasized a shift toward a growth mindset, innovation, and inclusion, anchored in more recent technological trends like cloud computing and artificial intelligence. This reimagination of what Microsoft could become in a new era created a shared language that unified the company around the path forward.

Visual tools like roadmaps, infographics, and internal campaigns can further reinforce a vision. When people see the journey and where they fit into it, their sense of direction becomes stronger.

Adapting Vision Without Losing Focus

Clarity of vision should not be confused with rigidity. In a fast-moving world, the most effective leaders remain anchored in their principles while staying responsive to change. A strong vision should evolve to meet emerging challenges, new opportunities, and unexpected shifts, without losing its core essence of empathy and humanity.

Scenario planning is one tool that helps transformational leaders prepare for a range of possible futures. By exploring different outcomes and rehearsing responses, they can make better-informed decisions under pressure. This approach enhances agility while preserving strategic direction.

Another key practice is **creating continuous feedback loops**. Leaders who regularly listen to customers, employees, and market signals are better positioned to adjust course without drifting off mission. These insights inform both the refinement of the vision and the strategies used to achieve it.

IBM's transformation (Sinha, 2023) is a compelling example of visionary adaptability. Originally known for its hardware, IBM recognized the changing landscape of technology and embraced a new path centered on software, services, and cloud computing. The shift required a reinvention of processes, talent, and culture. Yet, throughout this evolution, the company's commitment to innovation and client success remained steady. Staying true to its principles, while exploring new possibilities, IBM remained relevant and competitive in a rapidly evolving industry.

Flexibility with focus is a hallmark of visionary leadership. It allows organizations to pivot when needed while still moving toward their long-term aspirations. Leaders who practice this balance ensure that their vision continues to guide and energize their teams, regardless of external changes.

One might say vision is the heartbeat of leadership. It calls people forward, sharpens decision-making, and brings coherence to chaos. Rooted in values, made actionable through strategy and storytelling, and sustained by adaptability, vision has the power to transform outcomes as well as cultures. As the world continues to change, leaders who embrace vision as a living and evolving force will create a lasting impact, one step, one choice, and one inspired team at a time.

RESILIENCE: THE KEY TO OVERCOMING LEADERSHIP CHALLENGES

Leadership inevitably brings pressure, change, and moments of uncertainty. Resilience, or the ability to bounce back from challenges and keep going, becomes the force that sustains a leader's energy, clarity, and presence throughout that journey. It is the internal framework that supports perseverance during storms and keeps momentum alive when progress feels out of reach.

Resilient leaders respond to setbacks with determination. They recover quickly from disruption, remain grounded in the face of adversity, and project confidence when others look for direction. Resilience isn't getting through challenges, it's also growing through them. It enables leaders to keep their teams focused, motivated, and inspired, even when circumstances are complex or unpredictable.

Developing a Growth Mindset

Resilience starts with a mindset shift. Leaders who view difficulties as stepping stones tend to build stronger, more sustainable momentum over time. Challenges don't derail them; they spark curiosity and innovation. This approach is deeply tied to the idea of a growth mindset, or the belief that abilities and performance can evolve with effort, learning, and adaptation.

A growth mindset transforms mistakes into insights. When leaders actively reframe setbacks as feedback, they create an environment where learning is valued as highly as achievement. Amazon's leadership culture exemplifies this. Jeff Bezos often emphasized experimentation and rapid learning through his motto, "fail fast, learn fast" (*Jeff Bezos*, 2023). The company's willingness to launch bold initiatives, even when success wasn't guaranteed, has led to breakthroughs like Amazon Web Services (AWS) and Prime. Each failure served as a stepping stone, accelerating the pace of innovation rather than slowing it down.

Building this mindset requires daily practice. Embracing discomfort, staying open to criticism, and encouraging risk-taking across teams reinforces a culture where resilience thrives. Normalizing reflection and self-improvement creates a ripple effect that empowers others to do the same.

Emotional Regulation Under Pressure

In a high-stakes leadership environment, emotional clarity is just as critical as strategic thinking. The ability to manage emotional responses during intense or chaotic moments determines how effectively a leader communicates, decides, and leads under pressure.

Resilient leaders maintain composure by developing emotional regulation techniques that enhance focus and perspective. Cognitive reframing, for instance, helps shift how one interprets stressful situations. Instead of seeing a crisis as a threat, it becomes a chance to lead decisively and inspire confidence. Practices such as mindfulness, breathing exercises, and reflective journaling provide tools to stay grounded when emotions run high.

Indra Nooyi, former CEO of PepsiCo, led the company through dramatic industry changes with extraordinary emotional poise (CoFuturum GmbH, 2024). Her approach combined empathy with strategic sharpness. She prioritized connection with employees while navigating complex shifts in consumer behavior and global competition. Her ability to remain centered, despite the pressure, served as a powerful anchor for the organization.

You can't emphasize enough the importance of support networks. They play a vital role in emotional resilience. Mentors, peers, and trusted advisors provide perspective and encouragement when it's needed most. Resilient leaders don't have to carry the weight of decision-making alone. Surrounding themselves with strong, thoughtful individuals helps restore balance and reinforces their ability to lead with intention.

Building a Resilient Organizational Culture

Leadership resilience doesn't operate in isolation. It sets the tone for the broader culture. Teams often mirror the mindset and energy of their leaders. When leaders demonstrate strength, adaptability, and transparency, they create an environment where resilience is a part of the organizational ethic.

A resilient culture begins with communication. During challenges, clarity and openness help people stay connected and focused. Leaders who communicate honestly, even when the answers aren't entirely clear, build trust and unity. Transparency fosters ownership and collaboration, especially during transitions or crises.

Supporting mental health and promoting well-being are no longer optional, they are essential for organizational resilience. Encouraging work-life balance, offering flexible support systems, and addressing burnout proactively contribute to healthier, more engaged teams. When people feel cared for and empowered, their capacity to persevere increases.

Google's research on psychological safety (Poyton, 2024) highlights how resilience can be cultivated through intentional culture design. Teams that felt safe to express concerns, share new ideas, and take risks without fear of blame were consistently more innovative and effective. Leaders at Google focused on building trust through open dialogue, emotional awareness, and genuine inclusion. This foundation allowed teams to bounce back from setbacks with greater unity and creativity.

Leaders who embrace a "learn forward" culture redefine how their organizations handle mistakes. When failure is treated as a pathway to learning rather than as a sign of weakness, people are likelier to take initiative, share bold ideas, and adapt quickly to change. Imagine what such a collective mindset can fuel? It will bring about long-term adaptability and agility.

Resilience elevates leadership from reactive management to long-lasting influence. It equips leaders to stay centered when challenges arise, harness adversity as fuel for growth, and model strength that radiates across their teams and culture. With a growth mindset, emotional discipline, and a supportive environment, leaders shape organizations that thrive under pressure and evolve with purpose.

In a world that is quick to reward speed and adaptability, resilience is no longer a bonus trait, it is foundational. It enables leaders to rise repeatedly, lead consistently, and inspire confidence no matter how turbulent the landscape. When resilience becomes a way of being, leadership also becomes a force of lasting impact.

EMPATHY: THE LEADERSHIP SUPERPOWER

Empathy has emerged as one of the most influential and essential qualities of modern leadership. It elevates communication, deepens trust, and fosters a culture where people feel genuinely seen and valued. Far from being a soft skill reserved for moments of calm, empathy has become a strategic advantage in environments that demand rapid change, cultural sensitivity, and emotional intelligence.

At its core, empathy allows leaders to connect on a human level. It's the ability to step into someone else's shoes, to understand emotions, perspectives, and lived experiences without judgment. Leaders who embody empathy create stronger connections and cultivate workspaces where loyalty, creativity, and performance naturally flourish.

Empathy Builds Stronger, More Loyal Teams

People thrive when they feel heard. When a leader listens with intention and acts with understanding, they signal that every voice matters. This simple yet powerful behavior leads to teams that are more engaged, more loyal, and more willing to go the extra mile. The bond formed through empathy builds resilience, fuels motivation, and strengthens retention.

For instance, Mary Barra, CEO of General Motors, has consistently demonstrated empathy through her leadership. From navigating the company through crises (The Career Strategist, 2024) to initiating cultural reforms within the organization, she places a strong emphasis on transparency, listening, and employee well-being. Her approach has earned her the respect of her workforce and helped GM move forward with unity and strength.

Key empathy-driven behaviors include listening without interruption, observing emotional cues, and recognizing the individuality of each team member. Leaders who take the time to understand what drives and concerns their people are better equipped to align personal and organizational goals. This creates a culture where people don't just work for a paycheck, but contribute to a shared vision with passion and purpose.

Psychological safety is another product of empathetic leadership. When people know they can express ideas, voice concerns, and admit mistakes without fear, the entire team becomes more cohesive and collaborative. This environment accelerates growth and empowers innovation at every level.

Empathy Sparks Innovation and Creativity

Empathy plays a central role in innovation. By focusing on human experiences, leaders are able to design products, services, and systems that truly resonate with their audiences. Empathy bridges the gap between insight and action—it helps organizations see the world through the eyes of their users and deliver solutions that matter.

Apple's enduring success can be largely attributed to its obsession with user experience (JS, 2024). From the iPhone's intuitive interface to the simplicity of AirPods, empathy has been deeply embedded in the product design process. Steve Jobs once described design as "not just what it looks like and feels like. Design is how it works." This perspective reflects a deep commitment to understanding and anticipating user needs.

Design thinking, which centers empathy as a core principle, has gained momentum as a practical framework for solving complex problems. It encourages teams to deeply research user experiences, test early ideas with real feedback, and iterate based on emotional and functional needs. When empathy guides decision-making, innovation becomes more relevant, inclusive, and impactful.

Diverse perspectives further enrich this process. Leaders who welcome input from a wide range of backgrounds, disciplines, and experiences open the door to more creative solutions. Empathy, when practiced consistently, dismantles echo chambers and encourages curiosity. It fosters a space where every contribution is valued, making breakthroughs more likely.

Creating space for inclusive collaboration isn't just good practice, it's imperative to businesses. The most competitive organizations are those that understand empathy isn't a distraction from performance. It's a driver of progress, invention, and sustainable growth.

Navigating Difficult Conversations With Empathy

Every leader faces moments when challenging conversations are necessary—layoffs, performance issues, crisis responses, or conflict resolution. How one handles these moments can shape morale, trust, and long-term engagement. Empathy becomes the critical difference between a conversation that fractures relationships and one that strengthens them.

Leaders who approach difficult conversations with empathy do more than deliver information. They connect, support, and uplift. This begins with acknowledging emotions. Validating concerns, frustrations, or fears shows respect and builds a foundation for understanding. People aren't just looking for answers; they want to feel that their emotions are being honored and taken seriously.

Balancing honesty with compassion is another essential skill. Transparency builds trust, and when paired with a genuine sense of care, it transforms hard truths into moments of clarity and alignment. Empathetic leaders prepare for these conversations by anticipating emotional reactions, planning their messages thoughtfully, and focusing on long-term support.

A compelling example of empathetic leadership during a crisis came from Arne Sorenson, the late CEO of Marriott.

In the early months of the COVID-19 pandemic, Sorenson addressed employees in a heartfelt video (Mcgirt, 2020). He spoke candidly about the difficulties the company faced and the impact on its workforce, while emphasizing solidarity and commitment. His vulnerability, authenticity, and sincere concern deeply resonated across the organization and the industry.

When a leader offers solutions and support, it further demonstrates empathy. Whether it's helping someone find their next role, connecting them with resources, or simply being available to listen, these actions show that leadership equates to building and maintaining relationships. Teams that witness this kind of care will remain committed, even through adversity.

Empathy transforms leadership from transactional to transformational. It fuels loyalty, unlocks innovation, and builds cultures where people feel empowered and understood. In every meeting, message, and moment of challenge, empathy allows leaders to rise with humanity and lead with authenticity.

As the nature of work continues to evolve, empathy stands as one of the most essential traits for visionary leadership. It connects strategy to purpose, performance to people, and decisions to values. Leaders who lead with empathy don't just shape strong teams—they shape the future.

THE SYNERGY BETWEEN VISION, RESILIENCE, AND EMPATHY

True leadership thrives at the intersection of vision, resilience, and empathy. Vision charts the path, giving purpose and clarity to every step forward. Resilience provides the strength to stay the course through adversity, maintaining momentum when obstacles arise. Empathy brings it all together—connecting leaders with their people, ensuring that strategy is grounded in humanity. Separately, each trait adds value. Together, they create a powerful, unshakable foundation. Great leaders don't choose one over the other, they blend all three into every decision, conversation, and action.

To cultivate this synergy, start with a personal leadership vision statement that reflects your core values and long-term purpose. Build daily habits that boost resilience, such as reflection, adaptability training, and focused recovery practices. Strengthen empathy by listening deeply, seeking diverse perspectives, and engaging authentically with your team.

Tim Cook exemplifies this triad at Apple—balancing strategic vision with emotional intelligence and a deep commitment to inclusive leadership (Rampen, 2019). His approach shows that when these qualities work in harmony, leadership becomes a force for transformation.

The future belongs to leaders who can see clearly, stand firmly, and lead with heart. Vision, resilience, and empathy are no longer optional, they are the cornerstones of effective, human-centered leadership. When these three qualities come together, they create leaders who inspire, endure, and elevate those around them. Influence flows from the ability to anticipate change, navigate challenge, and deeply connect with people. The most impactful leaders don't master one trait—they balance all three with intention and integrity.

CALL TO ACTION

- Take a moment to reflect: Which of the qualities discussed above is your strength? Which one challenges you the most? Choose one practice to implement this week—whether it's refining your leadership vision, building a resilience ritual, or listening with deeper empathy.

Growth begins with small, intentional actions. The leader you're becoming is shaped by what you do today.

PSYCHOLOGICAL SAFETY

CREATING A CULTURE OF OPENNESS AND INNOVATION

> *Coming together is a beginning. Keeping together is progress. Working together is success.*
>
> — HENRY FORD

Imagine walking into your workplace each morning feeling not just physically protected, but truly free to speak up, take risks, and share bold ideas, without the fear of ridicule or reprisal. That's the extraordinary promise of psychological safety—an environment where employees believe that their well-being, thoughts, and creativity are genuinely valued. Unlike ergonomic chairs or safety goggles, psychological safety resides in the invisible realm of trust and respect. It's the assurance that a question won't trigger a sneer, admitting a mistake won't invite punishment, and proposing a daring solution won't be met with dismissive silence.

Yet traditional leadership often overlooks this vital element. Task-driven goals, hierarchical structures, and "just get it done" mindsets prioritize short-term outputs over long-term innovation. Managers focused on metrics may inadvertently silence critical conversations, leaving teams afraid to flag risks or propose transformative ideas. When leaders dismiss feedback, rely on rigid command-and-control tactics, or punish failure, they erect invisible barriers that stifle collaboration and erode morale.

Without psychological safety, organizations become incubators of conformity rather than hubs of creativity. Conversely, high-performing teams consistently highlight psychological safety as the bedrock of breakthrough thinking. When employees feel secure, they experiment, challenge the status quo, and build upon each other's insights. Ideas flow more freely, problem-solving accelerates, and innovations emerge organically, fueling both individual fulfillment and organizational success.

In this chapter, we explore why cultivating psychological safety is not merely a "nice-to-have," but a strategic necessity, and how it unleashes the powerhouse of innovation that every thriving workplace needs.

PSYCHOLOGICAL SAFETY: THE FOUNDATION OF HIGH-PERFORMING TEAMS

At its core, psychological safety is the shared belief that a team is safe for interpersonal risk-taking. It's not comfort, nor the absence of conflict, but the vibrant space where trust, mutual respect, and inclusivity converge to fuel growth. Harvard professor Amy Edmondson first coined the term, framing psychological safety as a critical antecedent of learning and innovation (Edmondson, 2014). Her landmark studies on healthcare teams revealed that when team members felt empowered to speak up, in reporting near-misses, questioning protocols, or voicing doubts, error rates dropped and patient outcomes improved. In contrast, teams lacking this safety net remained silent, perpetuating mistakes that could have been averted with a small question or clarification.

Understanding Psychological Safety

Edmondson's research underscores a vital point—psychological safety isn't creating a cushy environment, where everyone pats each other on the back. Rather, it involves a culture of being unafraid to share. Unlike comfort zones, where complacency reigns and people tread lightly, psychological safety invites healthy discomfort. It's the willingness to admit ignorance, to propose unorthodox ideas, and to embrace constructive conflict.

Trust and mutual respect are its lifeblood because team members know their contributions will be heard, valued, and debated, not dismissed or ridiculed. Inclusivity ensures diverse perspectives are taken into account during every conversation, which will enrich the team's collective intelligence.

The Business Case for Psychological Safety

The dividends of psychological safety extend well beyond warm fuzzies. Multiple studies have demonstrated that safe teams outperform their peers on key metrics (Panayides, 2024). With open lines of communication, problems surface early and are resolved quickly, reducing costly rework and bottlenecks. Employee retention climbs as individuals feel seen and supported. Employee turnover, which can sap millions in recruiting and training expenses, plummets when people trust their colleagues and leaders. Creativity soars as barriers to idea-sharing crumble, enabling teams to iterate rapidly and outpace competitors.

When Paul O'Neill became Alcoa's CEO in 1987, he shocked Wall Street by declaring that zero worker injuries, and not quarterly earnings, would be his top priority. Relentlessly focusing on frontline safety, his message was clear—every employee mattered and had permission to speak up about hazards or process flaws. O'Neill dismantled punitive management norms by taking personal responsibility for incidents, once famously telling plant executives after a fatal accident, "We killed this man. It's my failure of leadership." He empowered workers to raise concerns directly with him, even sharing his home phone number. This laser focus on safety ignited a broader culture shift. As teams collaborated to eliminate risks, communication barriers fell, and operational efficiencies improved. Over his 1987–1999 tenure, Alcoa's market value soared from $3 billion to $27 billion, and its annual net income quintupled, achievements the company's board later attributed directly to the trust and transparency O'Neill fostered (Garratt et al., 2024).

Psychological safety directly bolsters employee well-being. Reducing fear of negative judgment lowers stress, anxiety, and burnout. Workers no longer expend mental energy policing their words or hiding mistakes. They can channel that cognitive capacity into creativity, problem-solving, and genuine collaboration. The result is healthier, more resilient teams capable of weathering the slings and arrows of market volatility.

Barriers to Psychological Safety in Organizations

Despite its clear advantages, many organizations find psychological safety elusive. Fear-based management styles remain alarmingly common, with leaders wielding authority to enforce compliance, punish errors, and demand conformity. Under such regimes, admitting uncertainty or challenging directives feels tantamount to career suicide.

Cultural norms further entrench silence. In some industries, stoic professionalism equates to invulnerability. Vulnerability is interpreted as weakness. Employees learn to mask doubts, smile through confusion, and nod along even when they disagree. Meetings become performance stages rather than forums for genuine debate, and critical feedback never sees the light of day.

Leadership misconceptions compound the problem. Many executives equate control with effectiveness, believing that tight command structures guarantee consistency and minimize risk. But in dynamic environments, rigid control stifles adaptation. Innovation demands exploration, and exploration inherently involves missteps. Leaders who refuse to tolerate failure inadvertently create a culture of risk aversion, where safe bets overshadow bold moves.

Another obstacle is the illusion that psychological safety automatically emerges when teams are simply co-located or digitally connected. Physical proximity helps, but without explicit norms and rituals to encourage participation, such as rotating facilitators, structured failure "post-mortems," or inclusive decision-making protocols, the underlying power dynamics remain unchanged. High-status voices drown out conversations, while quieter, often equally insightful, team members are left on the sidelines.

Overcoming the Barriers

Cultivating psychological safety requires deliberate, sustained effort. Leaders must model the behaviors they wish to see. Ask open-ended questions, share personal missteps, and invite critique of their own decisions. A simple admission like, "I don't have all the answers, what do you think?," can open the floodgates of creativity. Structured practices also help, such as "start, stop, continue" exercises that prompt teams to assess processes candidly, or "round-robin" check-ins where every voice is heard before a discussion proceeds.

It's equally important to celebrate and normalize failure as a stepping stone to learning. Publicly dissecting what went wrong, and more importantly, how the team will adapt, sends a powerful message. It teaches that mistakes are not career-ending events but opportunities for growth. When the organization rewards curiosity and perseverance over blind perfection, employees feel empowered to stretch beyond their comfort zones.

Finally, embedding psychological safety into performance management and talent development systems ensures it withstands leadership changes and business cycles. Team collaboration and learning agility should be used as core competencies in evaluations. In this way, organizations signal that interpersonal risk-taking is integral to success. Training programs, coaching sessions, and peer mentoring can reinforce these norms, creating a self-reinforcing ecosystem where safety begets safety.

Psychological safety is neither a soft concept nor a one-time initiative. It's the bedrock of every high-performing team. Organizations can unlock the full potential of their people by making the business case clear, dismantling entrenched barriers, and instituting deliberate practices. In doing these, they drive extraordinary results together.

ENCOURAGING HEALTHY RISK-TAKING AND HONEST COMMUNICATION

Looking at Amazon's "fail fast, learn fast" paradigm again, we understand that at the heart of every breakthrough lies a bold leap into the unknown—a leap that is only possible when people feel free to take risks. Innovation demands experiments that may fail spectacularly. When teams learn to see failure not as an indictment but as a stepping-stone, they unlock a cycle: Curiosity fuels trial, trial yields lessons, lessons inspire new ideas, and the next iteration edges ever closer to transformative success.

Fear of criticism or reprisal can smother creativity before it even takes flight. In psychologically unsafe environments, employees censor unconventional proposals, worried that a misstep, or even a half-formed idea, will mark them as incompetent. As a result, organizations default to incremental tweaks rather than daring leaps. By contrast, when teams know their daring concepts will be met with open minds rather than raised eyebrows, they push boundaries, and sometimes shatter them entirely.

Disruptive innovations, from the smartphone to ride-sharing platforms, emerged in cultures where questioning orthodoxy was the norm, not the exception. Safe projects designed to protect existing revenue streams seldom yield big transformations. Big innovations require space for wild, untested hypotheses. Psychological safety is the oxygen for such daring pursuits, giving individuals permission to fail and learn faster, and keep trying for solutions that redefine industries.

Leadership Behaviors That Promote Open Communication

Leaders set the tone. Active listening, or truly hearing what's said and unsaid, demonstrates respect and signals that every voice matters. Beyond polite nods, it's paraphrasing to confirm understanding, asking clarifying questions, and reflecting the speaker's ideas and emotions. When employees witness leaders attuned to their words, they're far more likely to share raw insights.

Constructive disagreement strengthens decisions. By explicitly inviting dissent, "play devil's advocate", or "what might I be missing?" scenarios, leaders normalize pushback and identify blind spots. However, it's vital that such challenges never trigger punishment. Instead, they should be framed as contributions to collective wisdom. Over time, teams learn that disagreements are not career-endangering confrontations but valuable instruments of refinement.

Curiosity amplifies connection. Leaders who lead with questions like, "What surprises you about this data?", or "How might we do this differently?", shift the dynamic from directive to collaborative. They demonstrate that not holding all the answers, they encourage others to share theirs. This posture fuels richer problem-solving and deepens engagement, as employees see their expertise honored.

Creating a Feedback-Rich Culture

A feedback-rich culture turns every interaction into a learning opportunity. The cornerstone is non-punitive feedback, and framing mistakes as data points rather than transgressions. Rather than asking, "Who's at fault?", leaders should ask, "What can we learn?", and ensure that the focus remains on process improvement.

Embed simple rituals to encourage employees to speak up. Allocate time in meetings for a "Question Corner", where anyone can raise doubts anonymously or openly. Use quick pulse surveys to out concerns in real time. Celebrate "failure festivals" where teams present their greatest flops and share the lessons uncovered. Organizations can erode the stigma around speaking up by highlighting that missteps are prized.

Performance evaluations must reward learning agility, not perfection. Replace traditional critique-driven reviews with coaching dialogues focused on strengths, growth areas, and personal aspirations. For instance, ask employees to self-reflect on risks they took, what they learned, and how they'll apply those insights. When evaluations prioritize development over judgment, employees feel safer experimenting in pursuit of innovation.

Encouraging healthy risk-taking and honest communication is not a one-off initiative, but an ongoing leadership practice. It begins with a mindset shift, from protecting egos to cultivating minds; from preserving the status quo to igniting possibility. Leaders who listen deeply, invite challenge, and coach through feedback lay down the tracks where innovation trains can run uninhibited. When teams embrace failure as fuel, communicate candidly, and support each other's growth, they can transform setbacks into opportunities.

OVERCOMING RESISTANCE TO OPEN DIALOGUE

Even the most visionary leaders may think twice about implementing psychological safety. It upends conventional hierarchies, dissolves command-and-control instincts, and requires a level of transparency that some fear will erode their authority. Let us explore why resistance arises and how to dismantle it.

Why Some Leaders Struggle With Psychological Safety

- **The illusion of control:** Open dialogue feels like relinquishing power. Admitting ignorance or entertaining dissent seems risky when every decision looks like a bet against the clock or shareholders. Yet, real control comes from collective insight. When leaders tap into the full intelligence of their teams, decisions are better informed and more resilient.
- **Unconscious biases:** We all carry implicit beliefs about who "deserves" airtime. Left unchecked, biases can skew conversations toward familiar voices and perspectives, excluding fresh ideas. Leaders who

assume they know which employees are "experts" stifle diverse input and perpetuate groupthink.
- **The challenge of the ego:** For some, being "right" is a badge of honor. They hedge against dissent to preserve their reputation, masking insecurities with defensiveness. Yet ego-driven conversations discourage vulnerability and punish honest contributions.

Strategies to Break Down Communication Barriers

- **Model vulnerability:** When leaders share personal setbacks, especially those unrelated to work, they humanize themselves and signal that imperfection is acceptable. An anecdote, perhaps even unrelated to work, about a parenting mishap or a missed deadline can open the door for others to speak candidly about their own challenges.
- **Normalize "I don't know":** Cultivate a lexicon that admits uncertainty. Phrases like "I'm curious, what do you feel?" or "I don't have the answer yet" grant permission for exploration. Leaders who say "I don't know" invite their teams to co-create solutions and demonstrate that not having every answer is not a weakness but a starting point for collaboration.
- **Tell stories:** This has already come up more than once, but narratives forge emotional connection faster than data. Leaders can recount tales of past failures, moments when a junior colleague's suggestion saved the day, or a change that emerged from an unexpected source. Storytelling builds trust and shows the tangible value of open dialogue.

Addressing Team Resistance to Psychological Safety

Not just leaders, but even employees may be skeptical of openness, especially if prior cultures penalized candor. Here's how to earn their investment:

- **Acknowledge the past:** Openly discuss previous "culture wounds," or projects derailed by blame, meetings where feedback was punished, or leaders who shut down disagreement. Validating these experiences shows empathy and paves the way for renewal.
- **Start small:** Launch micro-initiatives, like a weekly "speak-up brief" where one person shares a concern; a rotating "meeting buddy" role that prompts quieter members to voice opinions; or anonymous digital suggestion boxes that gather unfiltered ideas. Each small success builds momentum and gradually shifts the norms.
- **Celebrate early adopters:** Publicly recognize employees who take interpersonal risks—whether in flagging an overlooked risk, challenging a flawed assumption, or offering a novel approach. Praise signals that the organization truly values courageous candor.

Leaders can transform hesitant groups into dynamic, courageous teams by confronting resistance head-on, modeling openness, and embedding safety into everyday rituals.

Psychological safety is not a checkbox to tick, it's an enduring commitment. Organizations that weave open dialogue into every process, starting from recruitment, performance evaluations, strategy sessions, to even hallway conversations, gain a lasting competitive edge. They attract top talent drawn to inclusive cultures, adapt swiftly to market changes, and consistently pioneer disruptive innovations.

CALL TO ACTION

- **Assess your team's current culture:** Reflect on whether your meetings, emails, and one-on-ones foster honest exchange or inadvertently reward silence. Consider a quick anonymous pulse survey to gauge comfort levels around risk-taking.
- **Model the change:** Deliberately share a vulnerability in your next team meeting. Ask a junior colleague for their perspective on a critical issue. Reward the person who offers the most candid feedback.
- **Ask for feedback, and act on it:** Implement monthly "voice sessions" where employees can submit concerns or ideas. Commit to responding within a fixed timeframe, demonstrating that every input matters.
- **Create a safe space for failure:** Launch a "lessons learned" ritual: After each project, identify what went well and what flopped. Document these insights in a shared repository, reinforcing that mistakes fuel collective growth.
- **Commit to consistent improvement:** Schedule quarterly reviews of your team's psychological safety metrics, such as participation rates in open forums,

anonymous survey results, the number of candid suggestions implemented, etc., and adjust your practices accordingly.

The payoff of psychological safety is nothing less than magical; for when it becomes the norm, organizations weather disruption by driving it.

BUILDING HIGH

TRUST TEAMS IN A DISTRUSTFUL WORLD

> *The best team is not the team with the best players, but the team that plays best together.*
>
> — JAMIE DIMON

Trust is the invisible currency of leadership—unseen, yet essential to every meaningful collaboration. In today's rapidly evolving world, we face a growing climate of distrust. Institutions once deemed reliable are being questioned, and skepticism has crept into corporate cultures, eroding confidence between leaders and their teams. Within organizations, even high-performing teams can falter when trust is absent, replaced by hesitation, defensiveness, and fear of failure.

Trust is imperative for success. Think of it as a foundational pillar influencing performance, engagement, innovation, and resilience. Leaders who fail to foster trust risk more than team morale; they risk productivity, loyalty, and the ability to adapt in uncertain times.

This chapter will explore the causes and consequences of trust erosion, especially in high-pressure environments. We'll examine the role of accountability in either strengthening or weakening trust, and how leaders can model trustworthy behavior. Finally, we'll outline actionable, long-term strategies for building and sustaining trust across diverse teams. Whether you're leading a startup or a global organization, mastering the art of trust is the key to lasting leadership.

HOW LEADERS UNINTENTIONALLY ERODE TRUST —AND HOW TO FIX IT

Trust is the foundation of any thriving team, yet even the most well-intentioned leaders can chip away at it without realizing it. In fast-paced environments where pressure is high and expectations are higher, trust erosion can happen subtly, camouflaged as thoroughness, leadership, or strategy. What are the consequences? Disengagement, low morale, high turnover, and a breakdown of team cohesion. Understanding how trust erodes and, more importantly, how to rebuild it, is crucial for leaders who want to foster strong, resilient teams.

The Trust Erosion Trap

Leaders rarely set out to diminish trust, but actions that may seem productive or protective often have the opposite effect. One of the most common pitfalls is micromanagement, often veiled under the guise of "diligence" or "precision." Leaders may justify constant oversight as a commitment to excellence, but to team members, it often signals a lack of confidence in their abilities. When people feel their autonomy is under siege, motivation suffers tremendously.

Controlling narratives or selectively sharing information is another subtle trust-breaker. Leaders might withhold context to "avoid panic" or manipulate perception, but transparency is a vital ingredient of trust. Teams don't expect to know everything, but they do expect honesty. When communication is filtered or overly controlled, suspicion replaces confidence.

Under stress, leaders sometimes become inconsistent in their behavior or decision-making. Shifting standards or reactive choices can leave teams feeling unmoored, unsure of what to expect or how to succeed. Trust thrives in predictability—when actions align with words and values hold steady, especially under pressure.

The Case of Uber: A Real-Life Cautionary Tale

A powerful illustration of trust erosion on an organizational level can be seen in the downfall of Uber under co-founder and former CEO Travis Kalanick (O'neill, 2024). Uber's rapid rise was matched by an equally dramatic fall, fueled by internal chaos, toxic culture, and a lack of transparency. Kalanick's aggressive leadership style fostered a high-performance but high-pressure environment. The company's culture prized results over respect, and information was tightly controlled. Accusations of sexual harassment, gender discrimination, retaliation, and ethical violations eventually surfaced, undermining trust, both within the company and among the public.

The damage was not only reputational, but operational as employee morale plummeted, talent fled, and regulatory scrutiny intensified. Kalanick's resignation was the direct result of the lack of employees', board members', and stakeholders' trust. His story underscores the importance of trust as more than a moral or interpersonal virtue; it's a strategic asset, and its absence has real-world consequences.

COMMON MISCONCEPTIONS ABOUT TRUST

One of the biggest misunderstandings leaders have is the belief that trust is synonymous with likability. While being approachable or well-liked can support a positive team atmosphere, trust hinges more on reliability, integrity, and fairness. Teams trust leaders who follow through, stay consistent, and make decisions based on principle rather than popularity.

Another second myth, one we have already discussed, is that authority automatically commands trust. In reality, authority can enforce compliance, but commitment, the emotional buy-in that fuels collaboration and discretionary effort, comes from trust. When people feel safe, respected, and treated justly, they invest more deeply in the mission and in each other.

A particularly dangerous trust-killer is the habit of over-promising and under-delivering. Whether in setting unrealistic goals, making commitments the team can't keep, or glossing over challenges, unmet expectations quietly chip away at credibility. Every time a promise is broken, no matter how small, trust takes a hit. Eventually, even the most visionary goals will fall flat if the team can't believe in the leader's word.

Repairing Broken Trust

When trust is broken, many leaders panic or fall silent, hoping the issue will blow over. In reality, acknowledging the breach openly and sincerely is the first and most important step toward restoration. A genuine apology, when warranted, demonstrates humility and emotional intelligence. It shows the team that the leader values the relationship enough to own their role in the breakdown.

But words alone won't suffice. Trust is rebuilt through consistent, aligned behavior over time. Teams need to see that changes aren't performative, but authentic and enduring. For instance, a leader who micromanaged may need to actively delegate and empower team members, even when it's uncomfortable. Trust-building behaviors must be visible, repeated, and reinforced.

Equally critical is the setting and meeting of realistic expectations. Over-correction can be just as damaging as inaction. Leaders must communicate clearly about what's changing, why it matters, and how success will be measured. Keeping promises, even in small ways, leaders demonstrate reliability. Each met expectation becomes a brick in the rebuilding process.

Trust doesn't evaporate overnight, nor is it restored in a single moment. It's built or broken through everyday actions, patterns, and decisions. For leaders, the goal isn't to be perfect, but to be intentional. They can create cultures where people feel safe, seen, and empowered by recognizing the subtle ways trust can erode, addressing misconceptions, and taking meaningful action to rebuild it. The most effective teams aren't the ones that never falter but the ones that know how to recover. And trust can make all the difference.

CREATING A CULTURE OF ACCOUNTABILITY WITHOUT FEAR: REDEFINING ACCOUNTABILITY

Accountability is often misunderstood, weaponized, or watered down in many organizations. Some see it as a synonym for blame—a finger-pointing exercise when things go wrong. Others treat it like an abstract concept with no real structure behind it. But in high-trust, high-performance teams, accountability isn't punitive measures; it's ownership. It's the act of standing behind your work, your words, and your responsibilities, even when the outcome isn't perfect. When reframed in this way, accountability becomes empowering, not intimidating.

Redefining Accountability

In effective teams, accountability is a shared value, not a tool for discipline. It's built on mutual respect and a shared commitment to the team goals. Leaders who reinforce that mistakes are not failures but learning opportunities create space for experimentation, creativity, and resilience. The myth that top-tier teams don't make mistakes is just that, a myth. Strong teams differ from dysfunctional ones not in having a spotless track record, but in how they respond when things go wrong.

Fear-based accountability, on the other hand, silences innovation. When employees are more concerned with avoiding blame than achieving results, they retreat, hide problems, or deflect responsibility. Instead of stepping forward, they step back, just when their insights are most needed. This fear-driven dynamic corrodes trust and stifles the very performance leaders are trying to enhance.

Building Psychological Contracts Within Teams

At the core of accountability lies the psychological contract, the unspoken but deeply felt agreement between team members about how they'll work together. It goes beyond job descriptions to cover expectations, support, and shared responsibility. The first step in building this contract is clarity. Teams need to know who owns what, what success looks like, and what the standards are for collaboration and follow-through.

Regular check-ins and feedback loops help strengthen this contract. Apart from just performance reviews or project updates, there should be real conversations where people can reflect, adjust, and realign.

Leaders who invite feedback and listen actively signal that accountability goes both ways. This dynamic also opens the door for peer-to-peer accountability, where team members respectfully challenge and support each other without always needing leadership intervention. That kind of horizontal accountability is the hallmark of a mature and self-regulating team.

The Case Study of Zappos and Radical Transparency

One of the most striking examples of accountability without fear can be found in the culture of Zappos (Richman, 2016), now acquired by Amazon. Known for its obsession with customer service, Zappos also prioritizes radical transparency as part of its DNA. Far from mere lip service, their value-centric approach shows up in day-to-day operations.

Zappos created an entire department, Zappos Insights, to give outsiders a behind-the-scenes look at how they operate. Through tours, training sessions, and Q&A opportunities with various departments, Zappos invites scrutiny. They invite being seen. This openness also enabled several external partnerships. CEO Tony Hsieh famously decided to give vendors complete access to internal systems through a dedicated extranet. This move went against traditional business logic, which held that vendor information should be tightly controlled. But Hsieh believed that trust breeds accountability, and transparency strengthens both.

This story reminds us why radical transparency can do wonders for team morale and the performance of the company.

The Role of Leaders in Modeling Accountability

Creating a culture of transparency doesn't happen by accident. It begins with leadership. And in any transformation, leaders must go first. This means admitting when they fall short—whether it's missing a deadline, making a poor decision, or failing to communicate clearly. When leaders are open about their own missteps, they normalize imperfection and encourage others to step into ownership rather than shame.

But modeling accountability isn't all about making public apologies. It requires a transparent follow-through. Saying you'll do something and then delivering on time, and with integrity, is one of the most trust-binding actions a leader can take. Every fulfilled commitment reinforces a culture where people believe each other, count on each other, and strive for consistency.

What's equally important is how leaders respond to others' attempts at accountability. When someone takes responsibility, even if the outcome wasn't great, leaders should celebrate the act of ownership itself. This separates performance from character and allows team members to grow from their experiences rather than fear them.

If you are a leader or looking to become one, praise the courage to speak up, the initiative to own a missed goal, and the humility to ask for help. These actions are the seeds of a fearless team culture.

From Compliance to Commitment

As we have seen repeatedly, accountability rooted in fear may get you compliance, never commitment. People may follow rules, meet quotas, or avoid errors, but they won't bring their full selves to the table. They won't challenge ideas, speak truth to power, or go the extra mile when no one is watching.

When accountability is rooted in trust and supported by clarity, autonomy, and mutual respect, powerful things happen. Commitment flourishes for one. Teams feel safe to take risks, own outcomes, and support each other through failure and success alike. Leaders don't have to force accountability, they simply inspire it.

For leaders, this shift requires patience, consistency, and vulnerability. It also requires redefining success. You may have to stop focusing on just hitting the metrics, in the process of building relationships.

In the next section, we'll explore how trust and accountability intersect with long-term strategy.

STRATEGIES FOR SUSTAINING TRUST OVER TIME

Many leaders make the mistake of treating trust like a milestone, or something to be earned once and then stored away. In truth, trust has to be a daily practice. It's built or broken with every interaction, every decision, and every unspoken response. And it's far more fragile than most people realize.

The "Trust Battery" in Action

Think of trust like a battery that's either charging or draining, moment by moment. A leader who follows through on commitments, listens deeply, and shows up when it matters gives that battery a healthy boost. On the other hand, ignoring feedback, canceling meetings last-minute, or making promises they don't keep depletes it, sometimes beyond repair. The "trust battery" concept reminds us that no single act defines our trustworthiness. Instead, it's an accumulation of small, consistent behaviors that make the difference over time.

Importantly, presence and consistency outweigh charisma. While it's tempting to believe that dynamic personalities inspire more trust, the truth is that reliability fosters deeper security. Teams want to know they can count on their leaders, especially when things get difficult. Grand speeches and big gestures may be good, but trust is born and reinforced in how leaders handle the everyday

This long-game approach means staying grounded in moments, not chasing milestones. So, think to yourself: How do you respond to a missed deadline? How do you handle a difficult conversation? How do you show up when nobody's watching? These small acts create a culture where trust is embedded.

The Case of Buffer and Fair Pay

One company that demonstrated sustainable trust is Buffer, the social media software company known for its transparency-first culture. From the outset, Buffer made a bold commitment, to make salaries public. Through an openly available spreadsheet, anyone can see what each employee earns, from the CEO to new hires (Richman, 2016). But the transparency doesn't stop there. Buffer also shares the exact formula used to calculate an employee's pay, factoring in things like job role, seniority, experience, location, and a fixed bonus for choosing a transparent salary.

This approach takes the guesswork out of compensation, removing the frustration and suspicion that often simmer in organizations around pay inequality. Employees understand how salaries are determined and why someone might earn more. In effect, what you get is a culture where fairness isn't a meaningless buzzword, but a practiced policy.

Buffer's model drums in psychological safety, reinforcing that the company has nothing to hide and that every employee can be trusted with the truth.

Trust During Change and Uncertainty

The real test of trust comes during transitions—restructuring, layoffs, a new vertical, or external crises. Change is inherently unsettling, but how leaders communicate during those times can either anchor trust or sink it.

The first key is clarity. When difficult decisions must be made, people need to understand the "why" behind them. Vagueness breeds speculation, which often leads to fear. Leaders should articulate not only the decision itself, but the rationale behind it. This doesn't need to include oversharing every minor detail, but it does mean treating people like intelligent adults who deserve the full story.

Next, is empathy. Change affects everyone differently. Some team members may feel anxious, others angry, and some might be relieved. Acknowledging these emotional responses without trying to fix or minimize them goes a long way in reinforcing trust. People want to know that their experience is seen and valued, even if the outcome isn't what they hoped for.

Finally, involving the team in the path forward creates a sense of ownership and shared purpose. Even if leaders need to make the initial call, they can still invite input, ideas, and collaboration on the next steps. This transforms change from something that's *done to people* into something that's *built with and for them.*

Maintaining Trust Across Remote and Hybrid Teams

In a world where many teams are dispersed across time zones and home offices, intentional visibility becomes essential. Trust suffers in silence. When leaders aren't physically present, their absence can be misread as indifference. This makes it vital to communicate clearly, regularly, and with intention. Video updates, open Q&A forums, digital office hours, or weekly check-ins—all help maintain connection without becoming burdensome.

But visibility alone isn't enough. Leaders must create rituals that reinforce cohesion. For instance, regular team huddles, collaborative brainstorming sessions, or informal coffee-video calls can recreate some of the vibe of an office environment. These may not all be "productive" in the traditional sense of the term, but they will build shared experience and relational capital.

Encouraging informal connection is also essential in maintaining trust from a distance. Teams that laugh together, share stories, and show vulnerability stay bonded, even if they rarely meet in person. Leaders can set the tone by being human themselves. Take the first step in showing that there is a face and emotions behind that screen image on your

Zoom call. Ask people how they are doing, or share stories from your personal life.

When leaders show up consistently, communicate authentically, and nurture a sense of belonging, trust not only survives but thrives, even if you don't share the same office space.

Trust as an Organizational Asset

Trust, when nurtured intentionally, becomes an organizational superpower. It speeds up collaboration, reduces friction, and allows teams to move with agility and confidence. But it's not static. It evolves, strengthens, and occasionally needs repair. Sustaining it over time requires leaders to stay alert, open, and deeply human.

There's no shortcut. No app, framework, or template will substitute the steady effort of showing up with integrity. Those who exemplify trust repeatedly reap extraordinary rewards like employee loyalty, innovation, resilience, and a team culture people are proud to partake of.

Ignoring trust can be a costly mistake. It fuels disengagement and workplace toxicity, draining energy from your team and momentum from your mission. The good news is trust is learnable, buildable, and renewable. A high-trust team becomes a self-reinforcing culture, one where accountability and care go hand in hand, where people challenge one another because they believe in each other, and where performance is elevated through purpose and psychological safety.

CALL TO ACTION

Now is the time to become a "trust architect."

- Start by auditing your leadership habits—could you be unintentionally creating ambiguity or fear?
- Then, have an honest conversation with your team about how safe they feel to speak up, make mistakes, and take initiative.
- Model trust daily by showing up, following through, and owning your impact.
- Use trust-building questions in one-on-one meetings, like "What's one thing you feel hesitant to bring up?" or "Where could I support you better?"
- Finally, make trust a shared responsibility. Ensure every layer of the team cultivates it.

Challenge: Over the next week, pick one work relationship where trust could be stronger. Take one intentional step to rebuild or deepen it, and review it constantly.

PART II
NAVIGATING CHANGE WITH AGILITY AND CLARITY

(HOW TO LEAD WHEN THE SCRIPT KEEPS CHANGING.)

LEADING WITHOUT A SCRIPT

DECISION-MAKING IN UNCERTAIN TIMES

> *It is not the strongest of the species that survive, nor the most intelligent, but the one most responsive to change.*
>
> — CHARLES DARWIN

Not long ago, leadership was seen as a matter of careful planning. You drew up a strategy, followed a proven path, and expected predictable results. But today's world moves too fast for that. Markets shift overnight. Crises appear without warning. Technology outpaces regulation. In this kind of volatility, certainty is more myth than reality, and leaders who cling to a fixed playbook quickly find themselves out of step.

The best leaders today may not have all the answers. However, they can act when answers are unclear. They know how to adapt, decide, and lead with conviction, even when the ground is shifting under their feet. This is the age of the *unscripted leader*: flexible, responsive, yet deeply anchored by a clear set of principles. They don't wait for perfect information. They blend instinct with evidence. They move forward knowing that action and progress, and not perfection, is the key to survival.

In this chapter, we'll break down what it really takes to lead in uncertainty. Learn how to navigate the fog, make decisions under pressure, and find the balance between gut feeling and hard data. Whether you're facing a sudden crisis or steering a team through constant change, this is your guide to leading when there are no guarantees.

WHY RIGID LEADERSHIP FAILS IN FAST-CHANGING ENVIRONMENTS

There are a couple of reasons why rigid leadership falls apart.

The Cost of Over-Planning

Exhaustive planning was seen as a mark of strong leadership. The idea was simple: control as many variables as possible and minimize surprises. But in environments that change by the day—or the hour—over-planning can turn into a trap. Leaders spend so much time creating detailed roadmaps that by the time they're ready to act, the landscape has already shifted.

Rigid protocols are the major culprit here. They slow down responsiveness at the very moment speed matters most. In times of crisis, decision-making that has to pass through multiple levels of approval can paralyze an organization.

Frontline teams know what needs to be done, but they're stuck waiting for someone higher up to give the green light. By the time permission arrives, the opportunity has passed.

During COVID-19, we saw how fatal this could be. Traditional retail giants, slow to move online, were overtaken by nimbler competitors. Companies that depended heavily on face-to-face operations, but hesitated to utilize remote services, lost ground fast. Meanwhile, businesses that gave their teams the freedom to experiment and make quick decisions were able to spot new needs, test new models, and evolve their offerings almost in real time.

Disruption as the New Normal

The problem isn't just that a big crisis like COVID-19 hit. It's that the world is now wired for constant disruption. Global events, technological leaps, political instability, and even changing employee expectations create a landscape where nothing stays still for long. Leadership can't remain protecting the status quo; it should be ready to reinvent at a moment's notice.

This complexity demands new skills. Flexibility has become a core competency, in that leaders must learn to operate amid uncertainty, making decisions based on incomplete information and adapting when circumstances inevitably change. The idea that you can "figure it all out" before acting is a luxury few can afford anymore.

And it's not even just reacting faster. One must also create organizations that are built for resilience, where people at all levels are equipped and trusted to respond, experiment, and learn. Leaders today must build cultures where agility, collaboration, and continuous learning are not buzzwords, but everyday realities.

Adaptive Leadership in Action: Spotify's Agile Model

Spotify provides a standout example of what adaptive leadership looks like in practice. Long before the pandemic, Spotify had already built its internal structure around flexibility and rapid innovation (Titov, 2024). Instead of organizing into rigid departments, Spotify grouped employees into small, cross-functional teams called "squads." Each squad operates almost like a mini-startup, with the freedom to decide what to build, how to build it, and how to reinvent when things aren't working.

This decentralized model proved invaluable during COVID-19. As user behaviors shifted with people listening more to podcasts during lockdowns, changing commuting patterns, or seeking new types of content, Spotify didn't need a top-down directive to respond. Squads were already empowered to spot trends, test new features, and make fast adjustments.

But Spotify's model isn't chaos; it's smart chaos. Coordination happens through structures like "tribes" (groups of related squads), "chapters" (discipline-based groups of people like engineers or designers), and "guilds" (informal communities around shared interests). These systems ensure that while squads move quickly and independently, they still share knowledge, avoid duplicating efforts, and stay aligned with broader company goals.

Another hallmark of Spotify's leadership approach is its embrace of a "test and learn" culture. Instead of betting everything on one big launch or strategy, teams are encouraged to experiment continuously. Small tests happen continuously, data is collected, lessons are learned, and ideas are either scaled up or scrapped quickly. This minimizes risk while maximizing learning—something crucial in a fast-moving world.

During the pandemic, this mindset helped Spotify explore new revenue models, like its push into exclusive podcast content and live audio features. Spotify could move with the kind of speed and nuance that a rigid, top-heavy organization simply couldn't match because decision-making power was pushed down to the teams closest to the customer.

What Spotify shows us is that adaptive leadership doesn't have to throw structure out the window. You can design structures that support flexibility. Teams can be trusted to own decisions, encouraging rapid experimentation, and making peace with the fact that sometimes you'll get it wrong, which is fine, as long as you learn fast.

For leaders, you need to shift from being the "chief decider" to being the "chief enabler." It involves creating environments where smart risks are encouraged, communication flows freely, and people have both the autonomy and the support to act quickly when new opportunities emerge.

In a world where certainty is an illusion, the ability to adapt has become the defining trait of great leadership. And as Spotify's example shows, when leaders create the right conditions for flexibility, their organizations thrive in uncertainty.

MAKING CONFIDENT DECISIONS UNDER PRESSURE

In high-stakes situations, leaders often face the daunting task of making swift decisions. The challenge isn't just external chaos but also internal cognitive strain. Understanding the neuroscience behind decision-making under stress can equip you to navigate these turbulent moments more effectively.

The Neuroscience of Decision Fatigue

Decision fatigue refers to the deteriorating quality of decisions after a prolonged period of decision-making (Berg, 2021). As individuals make more choices throughout the day, their cognitive resources become depleted, leading to impaired judgment and impulsivity. This phenomenon can result in analysis paralysis, where overthinking hinders action, or snap decisions driven by mental exhaustion.

Under stress, the brain's prefrontal cortex, responsible for complex decision-making, can become overwhelmed. This overload may cause individuals to default to habitual behaviors or avoid decisions altogether. Recognizing the signs of decision fatigue, such as irritability, indecisiveness, or mental fog, is crucial for leaders aiming to maintain clarity under pressure.

Creating Decision Frameworks Before the Crisis

Effective leaders anticipate crises by establishing decision-making frameworks in advance. Pre-defined principles will act as a compass during chaos, ensuring consistency and alignment with organizational values. Scenario planning, involving "what-if" analyses, prepares teams to respond to various contingencies, reducing the cognitive load during actual crises.

One practical tool is the OODA loop—Observe, Orient, Decide, Act—developed by military strategist John Boyd (Crowley, 2025). This iterative process encourages continuous assessment and adaptation, enabling swift and informed decisions in rapidly changing environments. By cycling through these stages, leaders can stay ahead of unfolding situations, making proactive rather than reactive choices.

Managing Team Anxiety Around Fast Decisions

Rapid decision-making can unsettle teams, especially when outcomes are uncertain. Transparency about the decision-making process helps alleviate anxiety. Leaders can build trust and foster a culture of openness by communicating the rationale behind decisions and acknowledging uncertainties.

Encouraging dialogue during ambiguous situations allows team members to voice concerns and contribute insights, enhancing collective understanding and commitment. Post-decision debriefs serve as opportunities for reflection, learning, and reinforcing organizational values. These practices improve future responses and also strengthen team cohesion and resilience.

Case Study: Starbucks' Response to Racial Profiling

In April 2018, two Black men were arrested at a Starbucks in Philadelphia while waiting for a friend, sparking nationwide outrage over racial profiling. CEO Kevin Johnson responded promptly, issuing a public apology and labeling the incident as "reprehensible." He flew to Philadelphia to meet with the individuals involved and local officials, demonstrating accountability and empathy.

Beyond apologies, Starbucks took concrete actions to address the underlying issues. The company announced the closure of over 8,000 U.S. stores for a day to conduct racial bias training for employees. This initiative, developed with input from experts, aimed to prevent similar incidents and promote inclusivity.

Johnson's approach exemplifies decisive leadership under pressure. By acknowledging the problem, engaging directly with those affected, and implementing systemic changes, he navigated the crisis with transparency and integrity. This response not only mitigated reputational damage but also reinforced Starbucks' commitment to its core values (*Crisis Leadership and 6 Effective Examples of it*, 2025).

BALANCING INTUITION AND DATA IN LEADERSHIP

In a world flooded with information but starved for certainty, leaders face a delicate dance: knowing when to trust their gut and when to lean into the data. Especially in times of ambiguity, mastering this balance can mean the difference between seizing an opportunity and missing it altogether.

The Myth of Purely Rational Decisions

There's a persistent myth that the best decisions are purely rational—cold, clinical, and based only on hard facts. In reality, leadership decisions are almost never that clean. True rationality assumes perfect information and endless time to weigh options, two luxuries leaders seldom have.

Intuition, often brushed off as "emotional" or "unscientific," is actually a sophisticated form of pattern recognition. Neuroscientists explain that intuition arises when the brain draws on years of experience to recognize complex patterns almost instantly. In fast-moving situations, these mental shortcuts allow leaders to make sound decisions without getting bogged down in analysis (Huang, 2019).

However, intuition isn't foolproof. Cognitive biases lurk beneath even the most seasoned gut feelings. Confirmation bias might lead a leader to see only the data that supports their hunch. Overconfidence bias might make them move too quickly without vetting alternatives. The key isn't to reject intuition, but to treat it as one valuable input among many.

Good leaders recognize when their instincts are surfacing and take a moment to ask critical questions: *Is my gut reacting to real signals or old fears? Am I ignoring inconvenient facts?* Knowing when to pause, question, and cross-check your intuition separates reckless action from wise leadership.

The Role of Data—But not Data Overload

If intuition is about speed, data is about depth. Data grounds decisions in observable reality, helping leaders validate instincts or challenge assumptions. In today's digital-first world, companies can track almost anything—customer behaviors, market shifts, internal productivity, even employee sentiment. But there's a catch. More data isn't always better.

When leaders are bombarded with metrics, reports, dashboards, and analytics, they can fall into decision paralysis. The irony is that too much information can make it harder to act confidently. The brain's cognitive load becomes overwhelmed, leading either to endless deliberation or to choosing the simplest, and not necessarily the best, path.

Effective leaders curate their data diet carefully. They focus on the metrics that actually drive performance, not the vanity numbers that look impressive but tell little. They design real-time dashboards highlighting critical KPIs and use decision trees to quickly weigh options without drowning in complexity.

For instance, instead of looking at a hundred customer metrics, a leader might zero in on three major ones—churn rate, customer lifetime value, and Net Promoter Score (NPS). These three alone can often tell you if your customer strategy is working—or if you're heading for trouble.

Data should inform decisions, not dominate them. A strong leader knows how to zoom out from the noise and ask, *What is the signal I'm looking for? What truly matters here?*

Synthesizing Instinct and Insight

Ultimately, great leadership is about synthesis. It's neither just intuition nor just data—it's the thoughtful integration of both.

Like building a muscle, this ability comes from repeated experience, or making decisions, learning from mistakes, and fine-tuning your judgment over time. Leadership muscle memory helps you recognize patterns faster, assess risks more sharply, and stay centered when the stakes are high.

Another powerful tool is surrounding yourself with a team that brings diverse perspectives. When intuition says, "go left" but two trusted advisors flag risks to the right, wise leaders pause and re-evaluate. Diversity in thinking acts as a guardrail against blind spots and biases. It doesn't slow down decision-making; it makes it stronger.

Knowing when the moment demands speed over certainty is a real art. Sometimes, waiting for the perfect information means missing the moment altogether. In these cases, leaders must make "best guess" decisions, using 70% of the needed information and trusting their instincts to fill in the gaps. Powell's famous 40-70 rule asks us not to make a decision, if we have less than 40% of the information, but not to wait for 100% of information, by which time the decision will come too late (Eades, 2021).

Case Study: Netflix and Streaming

As we discussed in Chapter 1, Netflix's transformation from DVD-by-mail to global streaming giant perfectly illustrates the power of blending instinct and data.

In the early 2000s, Netflix dominated DVD rentals. Their logistics were strong, customer satisfaction was high, and profitability was rising. By most traditional measures, there was no urgent reason to change. But Reed Hastings, Netflix's CEO, saw the writing on the wall. The future wasn't in physical, but digital media.

The data at the time didn't make an overwhelming case for streaming. Broadband internet wasn't yet ubiquitous, and consumer habits favored DVDs. Yet, Hastings and his team intuited a powerful pattern. Technology was accelerating faster than people realized, and consumer preferences would shift once the infrastructure caught up.

Despite initial resistance, even internally in the company, and public backlash against separating the services as Netflix and Qwikster, Hastings made the call to gradually double down on streaming. He combined early market trend data, observations of shifting consumer behavior, and a deep belief in digital transformation to drive the move (Rodriguez, 2018).

Netflix didn't rely on gut feeling alone and jump into the decision. After an initial foray, they tested assumptions continuously. Experimenting with small streaming pilots, analyzing customer adoption rates, and refining the user experience. Their ability to move nimbly, test ideas, and learn fast ultimately turned them from a DVD service into one of the most influential entertainment companies on earth.

Netflix's story underscores a huge lesson—playing it safe will not yield transformative leadership. Good leadership is balancing hard evidence with courageous vision, and then acting boldly when the right moment demands it.

In short, decision-making is not gathering the perfect data, it's blending intuition, experience, and hard data into confident, timely action. Leaders who master this balance will turn it into their greatest advantage.

A leader doesn't have to know the right answer, as much as make the best decision they can with what they have. Finally, moving forward with the courage of their convictions is vital. In a world that changes by the minute, flexibility, decisiveness, and honesty matter more than certainty.

The best leaders are explorers. They navigate the unknown with confidence, adapting their course as new information emerges, while staying true to their destination— their core principles.

CALL TO ACTION

Build your Unscripted Decision Toolkit and start strengthening your ability to lead without a script using each of the following:

- **Reflect:** Think of three times you defaulted to a rigid process. Did it help—or hold you back?

- **Create your code:** Draft a personal decision-making code. Pick three guiding principles you'll lean on when you're unsure.
- **Scenario practice:** Each month, run one "what-if" exercise with your team to keep flexible thinking sharp.
- **Reflect and adjust:** After big decisions, host short team retrospectives. What worked? What would you tweak next time?
- **Speak openly:** Your team doesn't expect you to be perfect. They want honesty. Share your thought process, especially when outcomes are uncertain.

The path ahead may be unwritten, but with the right mindset and tools, you won't just survive uncertainty—you'll lead through it.

ADAPTIVE COMMUNICATION

LEADING THROUGH CLARITY AND CONNECTION

> *The single biggest problem in communication is the illusion that it has taken place.*
>
> — GEORGE BERNARD SHAW

Imagine a leader with a groundbreaking vision—a bold strategy to transform the organization, elevate performance, and inspire innovation. But there's one problem. No one understands them. Meetings are confusing, emails fall flat, and their team, though talented, is disengaged. It's not that the ideas are flawed; the problem is with the communication. In today's fast-moving, multi-generational, hybrid workplaces, brilliant thinking means little if it can't be clearly and meaningfully conveyed.

This chapter begins with a simple truth—communication is no longer a "soft skill." It's the pulse of effective leadership. The ability to express, engage, and listen with clarity and empathy now determines whether a leader thrives or merely survives. In environments shaped by rapid change, uncertainty, and constant connectivity, communication has evolved from delivering messages to building connections. Broadcasting from top-down is no longer effective communication. Instead, it should be to create a space where dialogue flows, trust grows, and people feel seen and heard.

As we explore the communication edge that sets exceptional leaders apart, this chapter will guide you through four core shifts: adaptability—knowing how to flex your style across people and platforms; transparency—leading with honesty and openness; storytelling—making ideas stick through emotion and meaning; and presence—knowing when to lead digitally and when to show up human.

Leadership communication today demands more than talking; it calls for intentional presence, emotional intelligence, and the courage to connect.

ADAPTIVE COMMUNICATION: FLEXING FOR PEOPLE AND SITUATIONS

In leadership, communication is a living, breathing practice that must shift with every person, context, and moment. Great leaders know that one message delivered one way won't resonate with everyone. Instead of relying on a single approach, they flex. They read the room, sense the emotional temperature, and tailor their message to land with clarity and resonance. This is adaptive communication, and it separates those who simply speak from those who truly connect.

One Size Doesn't Fit All

Today's workforce spans four generations, from Baby Boomers to Gen Z, each shaped by different cultural norms, technologies, and communication expectations. Boomers often value structured updates, face-to-face interaction, and hierarchical clarity. Gen Z, by contrast, thrives on informal messaging, visual storytelling, and real-time feedback. A leader who sends a detailed weekly memo might earn respect from one group while completely losing another who prefers a quick Slack message and a meme.

Adaptive leaders recognize these nuances, not to pander to any one group, but to bridge the gaps. They take the time to learn how their people listen, absorb, and respond. The message stays consistent, but the method evolves.

Beyond generational preferences, neurodiversity introduces another dimension. Some team members may process language literally, need more time to respond, or find group discussions overwhelming. Adaptive communicators ensure accessibility by slowing down, offering written summaries, and allowing multiple ways to participate. They don't just accommodate differences—they anticipate them.

How Emotional Intelligence Shapes Communication Style

At the heart of adaptive communication is EI, emotional intelligence or what is otherwise called EQ (emotional quotient). Leaders with high EQ tune into their audience's mood, needs, and unspoken cues. They shift from pushing information to creating engagement. When tension is high, they lower the intensity. When morale dips, they speak with uplift. EQ empowers a leader to be firm without being cold, enthusiastic without being performative, and honest without being harsh.

Crucially, EQ also governs self-awareness. A leader who notices their tendency to dominate meetings can learn to pause, invite others in, and listen. This inner calibration, or recognizing when your default style may not serve the situation, is the gateway to more authentic and effective communication.

Listening as a Leadership Skill

Too often, leadership communication is equated with talking. But the most powerful leaders listen more than they speak. Active listening, which we have already dealt with, is a form of respect. It tells people that their voice matters, their input is valued, and their presence is seen. This isn't about nodding silently or waiting to speak. It means asking thoughtful questions, pausing before replying, and paraphrasing the speaker's ideas to show understanding.

Leaders who listen actively cultivate dialogue rather than monologue. They replace "Here's what we're doing" with "What do you see that I might be missing?" They model humility, curiosity, and openness. And when misunderstandings inevitably arise, they use simple tools like asking for summaries, clarifying next steps, or following up in writing, to reduce misinterpretation and reinforce alignment.

Matching Message to Context

Just as important as knowing *who* you're speaking to is knowing *what* the moment requires. Not every message is created equal. A crisis calls for calm authority and clarity; a vision needs energy and narrative; feedback requires tact and empathy.

Leaders who master contextual communication understand this terrain. In moments of uncertainty, they don't sugarcoat, they simplify. In moments of celebration, they elevate. In giving feedback, they shift from criticism to growth-focused conversations. One message can land very differently depending on tone, timing, and channel. A text might be perfect for quick praise, but inappropriate for delivering difficult news. A spontaneous video message might rally a remote team better than a polished email.

There is also a constant balancing act between being directive and being collaborative. During a crisis, decisive direction may be necessary. However, during planning or innovation, a collaborative tone fosters better ideas and stronger commitment. Adaptive communicators move between various modes with intention, always asking, "What does this moment need from me?"

Real-World Example: Sundar Pichai's Leadership at Google

Sundar Pichai, CEO of Google and Alphabet, offers a powerful case study in adaptive communication. Known for his calm demeanor and clarity, Pichai consistently models EQ in action. When facing employee protests or navigating economic shifts, he communicates with both transparency and restraint. He doesn't deflect tough topics. Instead, he names them. He listens to employees across the globe, adapts his tone to audience needs, and builds trust through consistent, honest engagement. He is also famously known for his use of the rule of three, wherein he dissects his answers or responses into three clear parts, which the audience can easily understand and take away (Gallo, 2023).

In internal memos, he explains decisions without jargon. In public forums, he humanizes complex strategies. And in team meetings, he creates space for open dialogue, reinforcing Google's culture of innovation and psychological safety. Pichai's leadership shows that clear, adaptive communication isn't just a skill, but a stabilizing force during complexity.

In a world where work is more decentralized, diverse, and fast-paced than ever, communication must be fluid. Adaptive leaders speak many "languages," not literally, but in tone, style, and presence. They shift with intention, lead with empathy, and above all, aim to be understood and make others feel understood. Also, remember, leadership communication doesn't have to be perfect; it's more vital to show presence and flexibility. When leaders learn to flex communication, they unlock the full power of their people.

THE ROLE OF TRANSPARENCY AND STORYTELLING IN LEADERSHIP

In complex times, people need information as well as meaning. Facts alone don't build trust. Strategies, on their own, don't inspire action. Leadership communication gains its full power when it is anchored in transparency and brought to life through storytelling.

Why Transparency Builds Credibility

Transparency in leadership is not telling everyone everything. It offers enough clarity, context, and honesty for people to understand what's happening and why. Too often, leaders default to delivering the *what*: "This is the change," "Here's the update," or "We're restructuring." But without the *why*, these messages land as commands, not communications. They generate confusion or resistance rather than alignment.

People want to understand the logic behind decisions, even the difficult ones. Sharing the *why* does not have to be over-explaining or defending every action. It means being open about values, trade-offs, and intentions. When employees sense that leadership is withholding information, trust erodes. But when a leader opens the curtain, showing the thought process, the uncertainty, even the emotional weight of a choice, it builds credibility, even in hard moments.

Vulnerability, used with discernment, plays a crucial role here. When leaders admit what they don't know or acknowledge a mistake, it doesn't make them look weak. Instead, it makes them relatable. It also sets a tone for others to speak candidly, ask questions, and bring forward concerns without fear. That said, vulnerability must be purposeful and not border on oversharing. You must bring the human side of leadership while staying grounded in responsibility.

Importantly, transparency does not mean alarmism. During periods of uncertainty like layoffs, market shocks, and leadership transitions, clarity matters more than certainty. The best communicators are honest about ambiguity without amplifying fear. They say, "Here's what we know. Here's what we're doing. Here's how we'll keep you informed." That kind of clear-eyed realism becomes an anchor.

Storytelling as a Strategic Tool

We have already talked a little about storytelling. To reiterate, humans are not wired to remember bullet points, we remember stories. We respond to characters, challenges, and transformation. When leaders communicate solely through data, goals, or policies, they miss the emotional channel through which people truly absorb meaning.

If you thought you must reserve storytelling for your speeches, you'd be wrong. It can be a strategic leadership tool that clarifies vision, builds purpose, and makes abstract concepts real. A well-told story can turn a strategy into a shared mission. It connects people to a larger context and helps them see their own role in the narrative.

Effective leaders craft internal narratives that answer three questions: *Where are we? Where are we going? And why does it matter?* The story might include moments of struggle, past achievements, or a customer whose life was improved by the team's work. These stories transform disconnected tasks into a meaningful journey.

Personal stories are especially potent. When a leader shares a real moment—perhaps a failure that shaped their approach or a customer interaction that moved them, it closes the distance between the title and the team. The story doesn't have to be dramatic; it just needs to be true and relevant. It must signal, *I'm not just leading this company, I'm living it with you.*

Creating Meaning Through Messaging

Too many organizations confuse messaging with branding. They develop polished slogans or values but leave them suspended in abstraction. Effective leaders move beyond corporate language and into substance. They take abstract messages like "innovation" or "customer obsession," and bring them to life with real examples, behavior, and follow-through.

One of the most powerful ways to create meaning is by connecting each team's role to the broader impact of the organization. Don't just tell people what they do, but remind them *why it matters*. An IT technician isn't just fixing systems, they're ensuring seamless care delivery in a hospital. A call center worker isn't just answering questions, they're preserving trust at a critical moment.

This kind of internal storytelling strengthens culture. It shifts the narrative from isolated functions to collective purpose. And when people see how their daily work contributes to something bigger, motivation becomes intrinsic.

Airbnb During COVID-19: A Study in Great Communication

A standout example of leadership communication that combined transparency and storytelling came in 2020, when Airbnb CEO Brian Chesky announced significant layoffs due to the pandemic. Instead of hiding behind PR language or delegating the message to HR, Chesky wrote directly to employees in a letter (*A message from co-founder and CEO*, 2020) that was widely praised around the world.

He was clear and candid about the scale of the cuts and the reasons behind them, explaining the company's sharp revenue decline and the strategic choices they had to make. But what made the message so effective was not just its transparency—it was the way it was told.

Chesky walked readers through the emotional and ethical dimensions of the decision. He acknowledged the human cost and described the steps taken to support those affected, from severance packages to alumni support. He used words not as rhetoric, but as honest expressions of the weight of leadership. He ended not with a corporate tagline, but with thanking the employees for their work and making it matter.

The letter turned a painful moment into a masterclass in human-centered leadership. Without avoiding responsibility, his message honored it. The letter strengthened Airbnb's culture, even in loss.

In times of pressure or change, people don't just ask "What's happening?"—they ask "How will this affect me?" and "Can I trust this?" Transparency and storytelling help leaders answer those questions. Together, they bring clarity, empathy, and direction to communication. They make space for uncertainty without creating chaos. They ensure leadership is felt rather than heard.

DIGITAL VS IN-PERSON LEADERSHIP IN A HYBRID WORLD

As workplaces become increasingly hybrid, leaders face a new challenge—maintaining clarity, connection, and presence across screens. Communication is no longer confined to conference rooms, it happens over Slack threads, Zoom calls, shared docs, and sometimes in complete silence through asynchronous updates. This shift offers flexibility, but it also demands intentionality. Without it, teams face communication fatigue, emotional distance, and cultural drift.

Communication Fatigue in the Digital Age

The early promise of digital collaboration tools was efficiency through fewer meetings, faster updates, and seamless workflows. But for many leaders and teams, the reality has been more chaotic. Slack threads spiral, inboxes overflow, and Zoom calls blur into one another. What was meant to streamline work can, if unchecked, create noise instead of clarity.

Zoom fatigue is real. It stems from screen time and the strain of decoding nonverbal cues in small boxes, the lack of transition between interactions, and the cognitive load of constantly performing "presence." Similarly, Slack and email, while convenient, often leave tone and intent ambiguous. A quick message meant to be neutral can feel curt or dismissive. Asynchronous communication, while powerful, requires even more care in how messages are framed, timed, and received.

Leaders must reduce digital noise and increase the signal. This means sending fewer, clearer messages; choosing the right channel for the right type of conversation; and encouraging teams to pause, reflect, and respond with intention rather than reacting instantly. One thoughtful, well-placed message often does more than a dozen scattered updates.

When to Show Up Live vs Lead Remotely

A central question in hybrid leadership is—*What needs to be said in person?* The answer isn't always straightforward, but patterns are emerging. Moments of emotional weight—like giving critical feedback, resolving conflict, or celebrating major wins—benefit from live, real-time presence. Even if "in person" means on Zoom, what matters is the leader's full attention and responsiveness.

Conversely, updates, instructions, and non-time-sensitive feedback are often more effective when delivered asynchronously. Teams appreciate the autonomy to read, digest, and respond in their own time, especially across time zones or focus blocks.

The art is in blending synchronous and asynchronous communication with purpose. For example, a leader might send a detailed update via email, then use a short team meeting to glean reflections or answer questions. Or they might record a quick video to convey tone and nuance when writing falls short. Across all formats, consistency is the key.

Instead of building on the quantity of communication, leaders must better its quality.

Maintaining presence across screens also requires rethinking visibility. Leaders in hybrid settings can't rely on hallway check-ins or casual drop-bys. Presence must be proactive—visible engagement in chats, regular video messages, office hours, and personalized check-ins. Authority doesn't come from physical proximity; it comes from emotional availability, clear direction, and trust.

Rebuilding Human Connection in Hybrid Teams

The greatest casualty of hybrid work isn't productivity, but connection. Teams miss the unstructured, informal moments, such as hallway chats, shared meals, and spontaneous brainstorms. These moments are from the fluff they're often hailed as. They build trust, empathy, and the social glue of culture. Leaders can't manufacture them, but they can design for them.

Intentionality is the antidote. Leaders can create space for informal interactions, whether through virtual coffee chats, shared playlists, or Friday games. Digital tools can also foster recognition and celebration. A public Slack shoutout, a surprise gift sent home, or a quick video note can go a long way in making people feel seen.

Pulse checks or short surveys, or one-on-one temperature checks, help leaders stay connected to team wellbeing. These can't replace conversations, but they can unearth patterns and signal where deeper dialogue is needed. Care and not surveillance is the end goal.

One powerful concept emerging in hybrid leadership is *designing moments that matter*. These are deliberate, meaningful touchpoints that reinforce values, celebrate progress, or realign teams. It could be an annual offsite, a live Q&A with leadership, or a surprise thank-you video during a tough quarter. These moments create shared memory and identity, even when people are apart.

HubSpot's Hybrid Leadership Model

HubSpot offers a compelling example of how hybrid leadership can be both human and high-performing. Recognizing the long-term shift to remote and hybrid work, the company reimagined its communication strategy to support clarity and cohesion without losing culture.

Rather than replicating office culture online, HubSpot treated culture like a product (Schmidt, 2019)—something to be designed, tested, and refined. They introduced flexible communication norms, prioritized transparency from leadership, and built digital rituals for connection. Team leads were trained in emotional leadership just as in tools. For instance, they were asked how to check in meaningfully, navigate burnout, and celebrate wins across distances.

Their approach didn't include more meetings or longer updates. However, being intentional was given paramount importance, using the right channel for the right message, making time for recognition, and showing up—digitally or physically, when it mattered most. The result was stronger engagement and a culture that adapted without losing its core.

In the hybrid era, leadership communication must evolve beyond presence to purpose. Being "always on" doesn't build trust, but being clear, consistent, and human does.

As this chapter has explored, the future of leadership is not louder communication, but smarter communication. One that flexes, listens, tells stories, and meets people where they are, whether across the table or across time zones.

The leaders who thrive in today's complex environments are the ones who connect the best. They understand that communication is not performance, it's presence. Adaptive leadership is choosing the right words for the moment, the audience, and the message. When empathy and clarity come together, trust follows. And trust is the true foundation of influence.

In an age of constant noise, the most powerful leadership voice is one that listens, adapts, and brings meaning to the message.

CALL TO ACTION

Level up your leadership communication:

- **Map your audience:** List three key people or groups you lead. How do their communication needs differ? Adjust your approach accordingly.
- **Audit your style:** Record yourself in a meeting or reread a team email. What tone comes through—intentional or reactive?

- **Practice a story:** Choose a real experience and shape it into a two-minute story that illustrates a leadership value or lesson.
- **Pick one digital ritual:** Try a weekly shoutout, a quick check-in, or a reflection prompt to maintain team connection.
- **Ask for feedback:** Once a month, ask: "What's one thing I could communicate better?" Then, listen—really listen.

THE ART OF MANAGING UP, DOWN, AND ACROSS

> *The way management treats associates is exactly how the associates will treat the customers.*
>
> — SAM WALTON

In today's complex organizational ecosystems, leadership isn't confined to corner offices or neatly defined hierarchies. The traditional top-down model is rapidly becoming obsolete, replaced by flatter, matrixed, and cross-functional environments where influence matters more than authority, and relationships are the true currency of leadership. If you want to succeed, it's no longer enough to lead a team, you need to lead across the entire web of your organization.

The evolving nature of leadership is such that the ability to manage relationships upward, downward, and laterally is essential. What ties all of this together is emotional intelligence, political savvy, and the capacity to read the room—sometimes literally, and often figuratively. You must know when to push, when to pause, and how to connect the dots between agendas, egos, and expectations. In this chapter, we'll explore how to build credibility across every level, communicate with precision, and move with confidence through the often-murky waters of modern leadership. In a world where no one leads alone, the ability to lead in all directions may be your greatest advantage.

If you are you ready to rethink what leadership really looks like in today's world, let's forge ahead.

MANAGING UP: INFLUENCING SENIOR LEADERS WITHOUT OVERSTEPPING

In the hierarchy of business, influence doesn't always flow top-down. One of the most underrated leadership skills is managing up, or navigating the gap between authority and autonomy to influence senior executives without overstepping. Now, this may seem like playing politics or flattery, but it really involves understanding the perspective of those above you and aligning your contributions with their priorities in a way that earns trust and amplifies your voice.

To do this effectively, you must first understand how senior leaders think. Executives operate in the realm of strategic vision. They're less concerned with the nuts and bolts of daily operations and more focused on the big picture, like long-term growth, market positioning, risk mitigation, reputation, and measurable outcomes. When you approach them, it may not be enough to say what you're doing, you will need to explain *why it matters* in terms they care about.

That means speaking the language of value. Instead of saying, "We need to upgrade the system," say, "Upgrading the system will reduce downtime by 15%, which supports our Q3 operational efficiency target." This shift isn't semantic—it's strategic. You're linking your ideas directly to company goals, showing you're not just doing your job but thinking in enterprise terms.

But not all executives operate in a similar manner. Each has a unique communication style, tolerance for detail, and decision-making pace. One leader might want crisp bullet point, while another might prefer narrative context. Some value data and others lean on instinct. Your job is to customize your approach. Observe their preferences. Mirror their pace and priorities. You don't have to turn chameleon, either; you can learn to be fluent in the language of influence.

Credibility, however, is the foundation. No amount of style can compensate for a lack of substance. Build yours through deep competence. Know your data better than anyone. Understand the broader business landscape, not just your slice of it. Preparation isn't making bulletproof presentations, it needs to be about being able to think on your feet, defend your perspective, and realign your tactics when challenged.

Timing and framing matter just as much as the message itself. Senior leaders are constantly bombarded with information. Dropping an idea, even a good one, during the wrong moment can cause it to be ignored or dismissed. Find windows of openness, such as strategy meetings, budget cycles, or right after a relevant event. Frame your ideas not as asks, but as value-adding opportunities. "Here's something

I believe can help us get ahead of X trend" lands better than "I think we should do X."

Influence also requires initiative. Striking a delicate balance between being proactive and presumptuous is vital here. Offer insight, not instructions. Ask for input instead of commitment when the stakes are still forming. That's how you bring ideas forward without sounding like you're leapfrogging authority.

One of the most difficult but necessary aspects of managing up is communicating bad news. Leaders don't want sugar-coating, but neither do they want panic. Bring up challenges early on, while there's still time to course-correct. Instead of flagging a problem in isolation, pair it with possible solutions. "We're seeing a 10% dip in conversion. I've identified three potential causes and have two test strategies ready." This is "no surprises" leadership. It builds confidence because it shows you're not just identifying issues, but also owning them.

Consider the example of Indra Nooyi at PepsiCo. Long before she became CEO, Nooyi was known for anticipating executive concerns and presenting her work through a strategic lens. She brought not just numbers, but also narratives tied to business outcomes. Her ability to manage up was consistent, deliberate, and deeply aligned with what the organization needed most. That's what made her indispensable (Bagwe, 2024).

In a nutshell, managing up isn't currying favor; it's bridging the gap between execution and vision. It requires clarity, empathy, preparation, and timing. Done right, it elevates your ideas and career.

MANAGING ACROSS: LEADING LATERAL TEAMS AND CROSS-FUNCTIONAL GROUPS

Some of the most critical work happens in an organization across functions, where influence is earned, not granted. In such situations, collaboration is more complex than command. Managing across means leading laterally, often without formal authority, in spaces where alignment is more important than hierarchy.

When you're leading peers or coordinating across departments, you can't rely on positional power. You have to lead through clarity, consistency, and the credibility you build over time. People follow peers when they trust their competence and believe in the value of their contributions. That starts with delivery. Nothing earns respect faster than doing what you say you'll do, every time. Reliability is underrated, but it's the currency of lateral leadership.

Influence across teams begins with shared goals. You may not have the power to give direction, but you can offer vision. Connect your work to a broader outcome. Frame initiatives in terms of what success looks like *for everyone*, not just your team. "Here's how we can all win if this project succeeds" is a powerful entry point to build cooperation. Vision, when grounded in mutual benefit, has pull, especially in environments where no one is obligated to follow your lead.

The biggest hurdle in cross-functional leadership is the natural pull toward turf wars. Silos form not because people are malicious, but because they're incentivized differently. There could be different KPIs, different customer views, different priorities. To lead across, you must reject zero-sum thinking, where one person's gain has to necessarily be at the expense of another. Collaboration isn't about whose idea wins—it's building alignment that lets good ideas thrive, regardless of origin. Start by asking what success looks like from the other side. Understanding others' metrics and pressures positions you as a partner, not a threat.

Great lateral leaders are fluent in the art of stakeholder alignment. They know how to map influence in terms of who matters, who needs to be onboard, and where the friction lies. They don't just push their agenda; they listen first, find the overlapping interests, and then frame the path forward in a manner that brings others along. Sometimes negotiation will work, while at other times you may need to use persuasion. However, empathy must be the driving force.

Conflicts are inevitable when teams with different rhythms and cultures converge. Marketing might prioritize speed and visibility. Engineering might optimize for precision and long-term stability. Finance wants predictability. Operations wants repeatability. Your job isn't to eliminate conflict but to make it productive, which means translating, not escalating the problem. If a team pushes back, don't assume resistance. Ask what's driving it. Often, there's a legitimate constraint or goal that, once identified, opens space for compromise.

Techniques for resolving friction vary, but the most effective is the simplest way—talking to people. Real conversations, and not emails or responses over a Slack thread, matter. Use one-on-one check-ins to understand concerns and joint working sessions to co-create solutions. Sometimes, all it takes is a human moment to reset a tense dynamic. Informal relationships, built on trust, not transactions, are often the real levers of progress in a cross-functional world.

Spotify's now-famous Squad Model, which we have already referred to in Chapter 6, is a textbook example of success in managing across teams. Squads are small cross-functional teams that operate with high autonomy and shared accountability (Cruth, 2021). No single person "owns" the others, but everyone owns the outcome. Success in this model doesn't come from authoritative control but from lateral leadership. Mutual respect, open communication, and a deep commitment to shared goals make the system work. Without those, the model would collapse under the weight of its own independence.

Managing across requires you to be both a diplomat and a driver. You need the emotional intelligence to navigate personalities, the strategic acumen to unite objectives, and the humility to know that influence isn't pushing your ego, but about outcome. In a world where silos slow innovation and collaboration fuels progress, lateral leadership is the engine that keeps modern organizations moving forward.

MANAGING DOWN: LEADING WITH EMPATHY, CLARITY, AND ACCOUNTABILITY

Effective leadership thrives on a beautiful vision alone. At some point, it will need to be translated into action. One of the core responsibilities of any leader is to serve as a bridge between senior leadership and the teams executing the work. That means turning strategic priorities into practical direction, without diluting meaning or overwhelming the team with abstract language. When done well, such a translation builds trust, focus, and momentum. When ignored, it creates confusion and disengagement.

To manage down successfully, leaders must communicate tasks as well as their context. Your team should not be guessing *why* a project matters or *how* their work contributes to larger objectives. Clear messaging that connects their efforts to company-wide outcomes fosters ownership. At the same time, strong leaders advocate for their people. They bring upward visibility to team challenges, bandwidth issues, or process flaws, not with the intention of shielding the team from responsibility, but to ensure they are set up for success. This dual accountability, to the team and the organization, demands consistency and integrity.

Creating a culture of honest feedback begins with psychological safety. Team members need to know that raising concerns, admitting missteps, or challenging ideas will not result in subtle punishment or reputational risk. That safety doesn't mean you neglect standards—it only means the presence of trust. When people feel safe, they don't hold back the insights or ideas that could move the team forward. Leaders foster this environment by listening carefully, asking real questions, and modeling transparency themselves.

Leadership is not control. Coaching produces stronger results than command. Leaders who empower rather than micromanage make room for initiative and innovation. This means letting go of the need to approve every decision or fix every mistake before it happens. It involves setting clear expectations, offering support, and then stepping back to allow ownership. When intervention is needed, it should be done with the goal of building competence, not authority.

Feedback is not a performance formality. It is a daily, active part of leadership. Effective feedback is timely, specific, and focused on growth. It does not rely on personality critiques or vague evaluations, but instead highlights behaviors, impact, and the next actionable steps. Just as importantly, smart leaders adjust their communication styles to meet the needs of each team member. Some people need structure, while others thrive with autonomy. Recognizing those differences is not favoritism or pandering to everyone, it is intelligent leadership.

Managing with empathy does not mean lowering expectations. Compassion and performance are companions. Leaders must be able to communicate standards clearly and consistently. Expectations around quality, timelines, and collaboration should be known and reinforced, not implied. But when setbacks occur, a leader's response matters. Reacting with blame will only drive fear and concealment. Responding with curiosity and resolve drives learning and accountability.

Holding people accountable is not the same as creating fear. Accountability is ensuring commitment and clarity. It involves difficult conversations when necessary, but rooted in fairness and respect. It also involves giving recognition where due, or publicly acknowledging success and privately addressing issues. Celebrating wins isn't boosting morale for its own sake. It reinforces the behaviors and results the team should repeat. In case things don't go to plan, strong leaders focus on the lesson, not the failure.

Leena Nair exemplified this balance in her leadership at Unilever and later Chanel. As Chief Human Resources

Officer at Unilever, she was widely respected for leading with deep compassion while still driving measurable results. Her approach was people-centered but performance-driven. She believed in unlocking potential, not enforcing compliance. Under her leadership, teams felt both cared for and challenged—a combination that created some of the most resilient and motivated talent pipelines in the company's history (Semuels, 2024).

Don't confuse managing down well with being liked. Managing down makes clarity, consistency, and fairness musts. It requires emotional intelligence to lead humans and the discipline to lead outcomes. In a time when teams expect leadership rather than orders, the ability to manage down with empathy and accountability is essential.

NAVIGATING POWER DYNAMICS AND ORGANIZATIONAL POLITICS

Power in organizations is rarely as simple as a reporting line. While organizational charts define structure, they often fail to capture the web of influence that truly shapes decisions. Successful leaders understand this distinction. They know how to navigate formal authority while engaging with the informal power grid that drives or stalls momentum.

This requires a clear-eyed understanding of influence. In many organizations, key decisions are shaped by people several layers removed from the spotlight, like a trusted lieutenant, a well-connected project lead, or the executive assistant who knows what's really happening behind the scenes. Being observant equals identifying these players. Who do people defer to in meetings? Whose opinion shifts the mood in the room? Who makes things happen, even when they're not in charge?

Leaders who succeed over the long-term build and leverage networks without resorting to manipulation. They offer value first—supporting others' goals, sharing credit, and making thoughtful introductions. These actions build goodwill and reciprocity without strings. They understand that relationships are not currency to be spent, but ecosystems to be nurtured.

Reading the room is part science and part instinct. Emotional intelligence helps you notice unspoken tension, hesitation, or alignment. Political intelligence helps you understand what those signals mean in context. This doesn't mean reading into every glance or tone shift, but it does mean being attuned to dynamics that others might ignore. The leader who understands not just *what* is being said, but *why*, gains an edge in timing, framing, and influence.

Playing the long game is a discipline. It involves restraint or knowing when to push for a decision and when to let something breathe. Timing can be the difference between traction and resistance. Don't consider strategic patience to be passivity; see it instead as purposeful pacing. Similarly, managing how you're perceived inside an organization is not vanity, but situational awareness. Are you seen as a builder, a critic, a doer, or a strategist? Perceptions often shape access to opportunities. Managing your personal brand means aligning your actions, communication, and presence with the kind of influence you want to have.

At the same time, navigating power and politics must be anchored in values. There's a line between political savvy and political toxicity. When influence tactics drift into manipulation, exclusion, or self-interest at the expense of others, the long-term cost is credibility. Ethics are not a luxury; they are a stabilizing force. When things get murky, as they often do, your values are the guardrails that keep your influence intact and your leadership trusted.

Standing your ground in a political environment does not require aggression. It requires clarity and courage. You can be firm without being combative. You can disagree without diminishing others. Effective resistance isn't loud, but anchored in facts, delivered with composure, and framed with respect. The most powerful leaders are those who can say "no" or "not yet" without damaging the relationship or the mission.

Influence rooted in trust is far more sustainable than influence built on maneuvering. People follow those they believe in, not just those who are well-connected. They support leaders who are consistent, fair, and transparent, even when things are difficult. Influence that is earned through integrity travels further than influence borrowed through proximity.

Sheryl Sandberg's rise at Google and later Facebook illustrates the complexity of navigating power with intention. She understood the hidden levers of influence and built coalitions across levels and functions. However, she also held to a clear leadership philosophy, focusing on empowerment, transparency, and long-term impact. Her political positioning of herself and the company was never detached from purpose. It was part of how she created space for others, not just herself (Thaken, 2023 & Sandberg, 2011).

Power dynamics are part of every organization. The goal is not to avoid them, but to engage them thoughtfully. When approached with self-awareness, strategic patience, and a commitment to integrity, managing politics becomes less about survival and more about shaping outcomes in a way that aligns with both your goals and your values.

Far from a vertical exercise, leadership today is a dynamic practice of connection, contribution, and influence in every direction. Whether you are guiding a team, collaborating across functions, or aligning with senior leaders, your impact depends on your ability to navigate the full system, not just your immediate span of control.

Real influence doesn't come from title or authority alone. It grows from trust, sharpened by competence, grounded in empathy, and communicated with clarity. The most effective leaders are those who adapt their approach without losing their values, who listen as well as lead, and who build bridges across boundaries.

CALL TO ACTION

- Start where you are. Map your influence web. Who do you lead, support, depend on, or hope to influence? Think in all directions—upward, downward, and sideways.
- Next, choose one relationship in each direction and invest in it. A thoughtful question, a well-timed offer of help, or a conversation rooted in curiosity can shift dynamics meaningfully.

- Challenge yourself to practice upward communication. Prepare one concise, value-aligned proposal for a leader above you. Focus on outcomes, timing, and alignment with strategic goals.
- Broaden your lateral reach. Start a simple, recurring coffee chat series with peers in other departments. Build shared understanding before you need collaboration.
- Finally, reflect on your political intelligence. Where are you naturally skilled? Where could more awareness or tact elevate your effectiveness as a leader?

Leadership is a whole-system responsibility. The more intentional you are about how you lead across, up, and down, the greater your impact will be.

LEADING THROUGH CRISIS

STAYING STEADY IN THE STORM

> *In a crisis, don't hide behind anything or anybody. They're going to find you anyway.*
>
> — BEAR BRYANT

In turbulent times, when the ground seems to shift beneath every decision and certainty vanishes like smoke, leadership becomes a test. Crises may expose weaknesses in systems, but they also reveal the character of those at the helm. When panic takes hold, reactive managers scramble to control the chaos. True leaders, however, do something radically different: They anchor themselves.

This chapter explores how resilient, emotionally intelligent, and visionary leaders survive and rise through crisis. They don't pretend to have all the answers. Instead, they lead with clarity, communicate with honesty, and inspire trust through steadiness. They understand that chaos cannot be tamed, but can be navigated with calm presence, adaptive thinking, and a clear sense of purpose.

The difference between a manager who reacts and a leader who responds lies in emotional composure and clarity of vision. Where others see breakdowns, grounded leaders see breakthroughs. They recognize crisis as a crucible or an intense pressure chamber that refines plans and people.

In the sections ahead, you'll discover what it takes to lead when everything is on the line, through emotional steadiness, strategic empathy, and the courage to unlock opportunity from adversity. In the darkest moments, even leadership can't control a storm, but it can find the calm within it.

THE PSYCHOLOGY OF CRISIS LEADERSHIP

Understanding how the mind operates under stress is essential for anyone who aspires to lead in times of crisis. In such moments, biology often takes over. The human brain is hardwired with a survival mechanism or the fight, flight, or freeze response. This primal instinct was useful when threats came in the form of predators whom we had to fight or run away from, but in boardrooms and business crises, this instinct can sabotage rational thinking and clear communication.

Great leaders recognize this instinct. Nobody can suppress it entirely, but we can learn to manage it. That's where self-regulation becomes critical. In crisis situations, leaders guide strategies and set the emotional tone for entire teams. When the leader panics, the team panics. When the leader stays grounded, others are more likely to mirror that steadiness.

Self-regulation is stepping back from emotional reactivity and choosing a mindful response. It means pausing before speaking, breathing through stress, and refusing to let urgency override clarity. Leadership in crisis begins with internal leadership, of one's own mind and emotions. The ability to shift from panic to perspective isn't just admirable; it's essential.

Emotional Intelligence Under Pressure

Daniel Goleman's concept of emotional intelligence—self-awareness, self-regulation, motivation, empathy, and social skills (Channell, 2021), becomes vital in high-stress leadership. Emotional intelligence under pressure separates leaders who merely endure from those who inspire and elevate.

First, leaders must recognize and manage their own emotional responses. Emotions like fear, anger, and frustration don't disappear in crisis. However, emotionally intelligent leaders don't let these feelings hijack their decisions. They name the emotion, understand its source, and refocus on what needs to be done.

Equally important is creating emotional safety for others. When a team feels secure, not necessarily in outcome, but in support and transparency, they function more cohesively. Emotional safety doesn't stem from false reassurances. It requires honesty delivered with compassion. It involves saying, "I don't have all the answers, but I'm here, and we'll figure this out together."

Empathy plays a critical role. Leaders who can see the situation through others' eyes are better equipped to de-escalate tension and build trust. They can anticipate fear isn't anonymous to authority, it, in fact, strengthens it by aligning leadership with the real, human experiences of the team.

Decision-Making Under Duress

Crisis compresses time and inflates consequences. Leaders often face making high-stakes decisions without complete information and under immense pressure. The neuroscience of decision-making reveals why this is so difficult: under stress, the prefrontal cortex, responsible for logic and planning, can become overwhelmed, while the amygdala, the emotional center of the brain, takes over.

In such a situation, avoiding analysis paralysis and decision fatigue becomes key. Strong leaders build frameworks ahead of time to avoid getting bogged down by every small decision. They empower trusted team members to handle tactical tasks, conserving their mental energy for strategic thinking.

Decisions need to be swift, but not reckless. That means balancing immediacy with long-term impact. The best crisis leaders don't just think about the next quarter, but consider how their decisions will shape culture, morale, and brand for years to come.

A powerful example of this kind of leadership is Warren Buffett during the 2008 financial crisis (ET Special, 2023). As panic gripped global markets, many investors retreated. Buffett, however, relied on his well-established team of advisors and the foundational principles of value investing. Rather than reacting with fear, he used the moment as an opportunity, investing in companies he believed would survive and thrive. His company, Berkshire Hathaway, emerged stronger, not just because they were financially savvy, but because they had a disciplined, emotionally intelligent leadership in the face of chaos.

Crisis makes and reveals leaders. It uncovers who has the capacity to self-regulate, empathize, and act with clarity even when the path is uncertain. The leaders who thrive aren't the ones who appear invincible. They are the ones who can acknowledge fear, remain anchored, and move forward anyway, carrying others with them.

COMMUNICATING EFFECTIVELY IN HIGH-PRESSURE SITUATIONS: CLARITY OVER PERFECTION

In a crisis, the quality of a leader's communication can make the difference between collective resilience and organizational collapse. Words matter, but how and when they're delivered matters even more. Amid uncertainty, people don't expect perfection. They crave clarity, truth, and direction. Great leaders understand that effective crisis communication is equivalent to creating stability through honesty, presence, and connection.

Clarity Over Perfection

Leaders often feel pressure to craft the perfect message—carefully worded, thoroughly vetted, and polished to a corporate shine. But in reality, speed and honesty often outweigh polish. A delayed perfect message can come across as evasive or disconnected, while a timely, clear communication, even if incomplete, reassures people that leadership is engaged and aware.

However, don't assume that you can be careless with words. A good leader embraces authenticity over artifice. People want to hear from a human being, not a rehearsed figurehead. They want to know what's happening, what it means for them, and what the next steps are.

During chaos, the structure of communication becomes a source of calm. Leaders should focus on four main parts of communication:

- information already available
- current steps of action
- what it will mean for the stakeholders, including employees and customers
- further channels of communication, and when you can expect to hear news next

Consistency in messaging creates rhythm and trust. People may forget the exact words, but they'll remember how they felt, and you want to keep them informed, considered, and respected.

Transparency Without Panic

In times of crisis, truth can be difficult—but it must never be obscured. Leaders often worry that revealing the full extent of a problem will induce panic. In fact, the opposite is, many times, true. When communication is vague, sugar-coated, or overly corporate, people sense it, increasing their anxiety.

Uncertainty breeds speculation, and speculation spreads faster than truth.

Transparency means communicating bad news with humanity, showing that leadership understands the impact on people, not just metrics. Avoiding spin is crucial. Euphemisms, buzzwords, and technical jargon disconnect the message from human experience. Terms like "rightsizing," "restructuring," or "realignment" sound clinical when people are worried about their livelihoods.

Simply stating, "We don't have all the answers, but we're committed to keeping you informed as we learn more," can be incredibly grounding. It acknowledges uncertainty while reinforcing presence and responsibility. Vulnerability, when paired with competence, builds credibility. It shows courage and maturity to admit limits while promising transparency and continued effort.

One notable example of this approach was Howard Schultz, the former CEO of Starbucks. During the 2008 economic downturn, Schultz returned as CEO amidst falling stock prices and low employee morale. He faced significant pressure from Wall Street to cut Starbucks' healthcare benefits (Schultz, 2010), which at the time cost the company approximately $300 million annually. Despite the financial incentive, he stood firm in his belief that maintaining healthcare for employees—those working at least 20 hours a week—was essential to the company's values. In one instance, an institutional investor contacted him, pointing out that the economic climate gave him the perfect opportunity to eliminate the benefit without backlash. Schultz responded by communicating that while he could find ways to reduce costs in other areas, cutting healthcare would undermine the trust and integrity the company had spent nearly four decades building. He made it clear that if shareholders prioritized short-term gains over the company's principles, they were free to divest. For Schultz, leadership was not solely linked to profitability—it was about upholding values, preserving the company's culture, and doing work that held meaning and earned respect. He emphasized the importance of standing firm in one's beliefs, even in the face of external pressure.

Two-Way Communication: Listening in Crisis

Top-down communication without listening is dangerously incomplete. Great leaders understand that insight doesn't only come from strategy rooms, but from the ground, where real-time experience meets real-world problems.

Creating channels for feedback like anonymous surveys, town halls, Q&A sessions, and even open-door digital policies helps gather "ground intelligence." These channels offer perspective and signal respect that "We want to hear from you. We value your experience. We are not above learning."

One of the most powerful tools in this process is empathetic listening. When a team member expresses fear, frustration, or fatigue, a leader's job isn't to fix the emotion but to honor it. Listening empathetically means staying present, validating feelings, and resisting the urge to interrupt or defend. This is not weakness; it's leadership grounded in human connection.

Crucially, silence from leadership in a crisis often causes more damage than mistakes. When leaders go quiet, people don't assume thoughtfulness, they assume indifference or fear. In the absence of clear messaging, people fill the void with rumors, misinformation, and worst-case assumptions.

Leaders don't need to speak constantly, but they must speak *consistently*. Even a simple message like, "We're working through the situation and will update you tomorrow at noon," provides a sense of security. It creates predictability in unpredictable times.

In a crisis, good communication is not saying the perfect thing, but saying the right thing, at the right time, with honesty and heart. Leaders who communicate clearly, listen empathetically, and show up consistently build cultures of trust that endure long after the crisis has passed.

TURNING CRISES INTO OPPORTUNITIES FOR TRANSFORMATION

In every crisis lies a hidden crossroads—one path leads to breakdown, the other to breakthrough. While the immediate instinct is often to stabilize and recover, the most effective leaders look further. They ask: *What can we build from this?* They recognize that crises, while disruptive and often painful, are also powerful pattern interrupters, carrying within them the power to shake old assumptions, expose weak points, and force a reevaluation of priorities.

Reframing the Narrative

The first step in turning crisis into opportunity is reframing the narrative. Rather than viewing the crisis solely as a threat, visionary leaders see it as a catalyst for necessary change. This reframing doesn't ignore hardship or minimize risk; it simply broadens the lens. It shifts the question from "How do we survive this?" to "How do we emerge stronger, better aligned, and more relevant?"

A strong vision plays a pivotal role here. It becomes the stabilizing force in chaos, a North Star that gives people meaning, focus, and hope. When people understand what they are working toward, even uncertainty becomes bearable. Leaders who communicate a compelling vision during a crisis energize their teams through purposeful direction.

Strategic Adaptation and Innovation

Crises often demand rapid shifts, but those shifts can spark innovation if leaders allow space for experimentation and learning. Fear can either freeze an organization or unlock creative energy. Smart leaders choose the latter, giving teams permission to test, pivot, and iterate in real time.

This strategic adaptability was exemplified by Satya Nadella at Microsoft during the early months of the COVID-19 pandemic. As global workforces went remote almost overnight, Nadella's leadership was marked by both rapid response and long-term vision. While Microsoft Teams became a vital tool for immediate remote collaboration, Nadella was already thinking beyond just video calls and chat.

In 2021, amidst ongoing global uncertainty, Microsoft launched Microsoft Viva (Nadella, 2021)—an employee experience platform built directly into Microsoft Teams. Viva was a product, born out of a deeper transformation. Nadella recognized that the crisis had fundamentally altered how people work, what they expect from employers, and how organizations must support employee well-being, engagement, and growth.

Viva brought together internal communication, learning and development, well-being insights, and knowledge sharing—all within the flow of daily work. It put people at the center of business systems. In doing so, Nadella not only addressed the current disruption but also reimagined the future of work in a way that positioned Microsoft as a thought leader, not just a service provider.

Through Viva, Nadella demonstrated how leaders can use a crisis as an opportunity to innovate at the intersection of technology and human needs. It highlights surviving the moment and building a more resilient, adaptive, and people-focused future. What was the result? Microsoft adapted and grew stronger, solidifying its place in the evolving digital workplace and setting a tone of confidence and agility.

Leaders who foster a culture that embraces change empower their people to take initiative, challenge outdated norms, and build new solutions without waiting for perfect conditions. Crisis creates a kind of temporary immunity from bureaucracy, and if used wisely, that window can lead to lasting breakthroughs.

Building Long-Term Resilience

The final, and perhaps most important, step is embedding the lessons learned into the organization's DNA. Too often, once a crisis passes, companies revert to their old habits, failing to institutionalize the progress they made under pressure.

Resilient leaders take a different approach. They use the post-crisis period to review decisions, assess outcomes, and codify best practices. What worked under pressure? What weaknesses were exposed? What new behaviors or systems emerged that should be preserved?

This is how new norms take root. It could mean faster decision-making processes, increased transparency, remote work flexibility, or more inclusive communication channels. As that, the organization evolves, leadership practices, too, must adapt. Emotional intelligence, real-time communication, and cross-functional agility shouldn't be temporary crisis tools, but should become standard elements of leadership.

The post-crisis leader emerges stronger, more capable, wiser, and more human. In turning crises into opportunities, leaders transform more than the companies they are leading, they transform themselves. They step beyond reaction, into reinvention, proving that while crises may shake the foundation, they also clear the way for something bolder, more adaptive, and more enduring to be built.

People don't look for flawless decision-makers, they seek leaders who are present, grounded, and human. True crisis leadership means showing up with clarity, composure, and connection when others feel lost. It's the quiet confidence that steadies a room, the empathy that defuses tension, and the courage to act even when the outcome is uncertain.

The leaders who thrive during crisis don't aim to return to "business as usual." Instead, they use disruption as a chance to reimagine, rebuild, and emerge stronger. They make space for innovation, listen with intent, and create cultures that can weather future storms, not through control, but via trust, communication, and adaptability.

CALL TO ACTION

Your crisis leadership blueprint:

- **Name your triggers:** Identify what throws you off-center under pressure. How do you typically react? What techniques can help you self-regulate?
- **Craft a clarity message:** Develop a three-point message you can use in any crisis, focusing on *what's happening, what matters now,* and *what comes next*.
- **Build feedback loops:** Set up or test one system, like a weekly pulse survey or open office hour, to gather real-time input from your team.
- **Spot opportunity:** Reflect on a recent challenge. What unexpected opportunity did, or could, emerge from that moment of disruption?

Crisis leadership is a mindset. So, start building yours now.

PART III
THE FUTURE OF LEADERSHIP AND YOUR LASTING IMPACT

(HOW TO FUTURE-PROOF YOUR LEADERSHIP AND LEAVE A MEANINGFUL LEGACY.)

THE FUTURE OF LEADERSHIP

AI, AUTOMATION, AND THE HUMAN FACTOR

> *Artificial Intelligence, deep learning, machine learning—whatever you're doing if you don't understand it—learn it. Because otherwise, you're going to be a dinosaur within 3 years.*
>
> — MARK CUBAN

The age of intelligent machines is no longer a distant future, it's here, reshaping industries, redefining roles, and rewriting the rules of leadership. As AI and automation streamline operations, forecast outcomes, and make split-second decisions, the question is no longer what can machines do, but rather, what must humans do differently?

In this era of digital transformation, the value of purely technical leadership is declining. What once were considered "soft skills," like emotional intelligence, ethical judgment, and nuanced decision-making, are fast becoming the hardest currency of effective leadership. When algorithms can optimize processes better than people, the human edge lies in empathy, adaptability, and vision. Leadership is not being replaced by AI; it's being redefined by it.

Gone are the days of command-and-control leadership. Today's high-performing leaders are guides and coaches, who are adept at using emotional insight and a collaborative spirit to get past challenges. It's no longer just how fast we can move, but how wisely and responsibly we choose to.

Companies like Google, Microsoft, and Amazon are embedding AI deeply into their operations, automating everything from logistics to customer service. Yet, even in these tech-driven giants, the leaders making the greatest impact are those who blend technological advancements with human-centric values and understand that machines may drive the systems, but people still drive the mission.

As we stand at the intersection of technological efficiency and human empathy, leadership demands a new kind of emotional intelligence, which is authentic. In the following sections, we'll explore how this new leadership model is not only surviving but thriving in the machine age.

HOW TECHNOLOGY IS RESHAPING LEADERSHIP ROLES

Artificial intelligence is the silent engine running behind the scenes of decision-making, logistics, customer engagement, and productivity tracking. As machines take over the tasks once considered core managerial duties, the very definition of leadership is undergoing a seismic shift.

The Automation of Managerial Tasks

Traditional management relied heavily on overseeing day-to-day operations like tracking employee performance, building schedules, managing resources, and analyzing metrics. These responsibilities were once time-consuming and demanded constant attention. Now, AI-powered dashboards and automation tools are transforming these tasks into background functions.

Performance metrics update in real time now, not at the end of a quarter. Similarly, scheduling software adapts dynamically based on workload and availability. Predictive analytics can now forecast customer behavior, supply chain risks, and even potential employee burnout before they occur. Leaders no longer need to wade through endless spreadsheets or manually balance workloads, but have decision-support systems that do the heavy lifting.

This evolution allows modern leaders to shift from being task-doers to becoming strategic visionaries. When technology manages the "what" and "how," leaders are freed to focus on the "why" and "what's next." The question to ask is no longer, "How do I control this process?" but rather, "How do I guide this organization through uncertainty and change with purpose?"

New Skills for the Digital-Age Leader

In this transformed environment, a new set of leadership competencies is emerging. Tech literacy is essential, not in the sense of coding or engineering, but in understanding the capabilities, limitations, and ethical implications of digital tools. Leaders must be able to interpret the data their systems produce, recognize patterns, and translate numbers into meaningful strategy.

Crucially, the modern leader must be agile in choosing when to trust the machine and when to rely on human judgment. While AI can optimize performance, it lacks context, empathy, and nuance, which are qualities leaders must provide to ensure decisions align with human values and organizational culture.

Redefining the Leader's Value Proposition

If machines can handle the tasks leaders once prided themselves on, what remains at the core of leadership? The answer lies in the distinctly human traits that technology cannot replicate, like trust, ethical judgment, inspiration, and empathy.

The leader's role is evolving into one of guiding human teams in an environment increasingly defined by non-human actors. Strategic decisions are no longer made in isolation but in real-time, supported by a continuous flow of machine-generated insights. This dynamic demands emotional intelligence, moral clarity, and the ability to connect disparate perspectives into a coherent actionable path.

Furthermore, the leader is no longer the gatekeeper of information. In a world of open data and collaborative platforms, leadership today must facilitate action, align teams, and nurture innovation rather than hoarding knowledge.

Case Study: Amazon and Machine-Led Warehousing

At Amazon's fulfillment centers, we see a striking example of this new leadership paradigm in action. Robots and AI systems oversee inventory management, order picking, and logistics, optimizing efficiency at scales no human manager can match (Yolga, 2023). However, human supervisors are far from obsolete. Their roles have shifted toward team morale, conflict resolution, and process improvement.

These supervisors are expected to understand both the technical systems and the human dynamics of their teams. They serve as translators between two worlds, ensuring the robots stay on track and the people feel valued, safe, and empowered. This hybrid role of being technologically fluent, emotionally intelligent, and strategically grounded is the blueprint for future leadership.

As machines continue to advance, the competitive edge will belong not to those who resist the change, but to those who evolve with it. Leaders will need to understand that while technology can drive efficiency, only humans can drive meaning.

THE ENDURING VALUE OF EMOTIONAL INTELLIGENCE AND HUMAN JUDGMENT

As the digital tide rises, many fear that machines will replace human leaders altogether. But even the most advanced AI lacks what is increasingly vital in leadership, which are emotional intelligence and human judgment. Far from nostalgic relics of a bygone era, these are the glue holding modern organizations together in times of uncertainty and rapid change.

Empathy and Intuition in Leadership

Artificial intelligence can process billions of data points, but it cannot feel. It cannot sense the quiet hesitation in a team member's voice, nor can it detect the fatigue behind a smile in a video call. Emotional nuance is not programmable. It is lived, experienced, and interpreted through intuition, something uniquely human.

Leaders must often navigate situations where data is incomplete, conflicting, or simply misleading. In those moments, empathy and intuition serve as internal compasses. They help leaders read between the lines, understand unspoken concerns, and respond in ways that foster trust and motivation.

No machine can truly inspire. Algorithms do not mentor. Conflict resolution, motivation, and the building of psychological safety remain firmly in human hands. A great leader sees not just a team, but individuals with stories, fears, and potential. AI might optimize a process, but it cannot look someone in the eyes and say, "I believe in you."

Human Judgment in the Age of Algorithms

AI excels in data-rich, pattern-heavy environments, but the same carries risks. Algorithms reflect the biases of their training data and the assumptions of their creators. They lack contextual awareness, cultural sensitivity, and ethical discernment. They don't understand nuance, and they don't ask critical questions.

This is where human judgment reasserts its value. Leaders must know when to trust AI and when to override it. The "human override" button is a fail-safe and a critical responsibility. Blindly following machine recommendations can lead to disastrous outcomes, especially when decisions impact people's lives, dignity, or rights.

Higher-order thinking or the ability to anticipate unintended consequences and ethical implications, is still beyond AI's reach. Experience, and not data alone, teaches a leader when a decision may look right on a spreadsheet but feel wrong in practice.

Coaching, Mentoring, and Meaning-Making

In a world where processes are increasingly automated, people are looking for more than efficiency. They are seeking meaning. They want to know that their work matters, that they belong, and that their leaders see them not as cogs in a machine, but as whole human beings.

This is where the leader becomes a sense-maker, someone who can help individuals and teams understand their place in the larger picture, especially during times of transformation. A coach, mentor, or guide is a necessity.

Even in highly digitized environments, people resist being led by algorithms. They want a human face on their journey. Leaders who invest in coaching, engage in meaningful conversations, and ask not just "what's your output?" but "what's your growth?"—these are the ones building resilient, innovative, and loyal teams.

Real-World Example: Lindsay-Rae McIntyre at Microsoft

Microsoft's chief diversity officer, Lindsay-Rae McIntyre, is at the forefront of this human-centric leadership evolution. While Microsoft increasingly integrates AI into its products and internal operations, McIntyre and her team focus on embedding inclusion practices at every level of development (Kelly, 2024). Her role is a powerful reminder that leadership is not just managing systems—it's about shaping culture.

Advocating for better representation in AI research and development, McIntyre is ensuring that technological progress is not divorced from ethical responsibility. Her work exemplifies the modern leader's role, which is to influence not just *what* technology does, but *how* and *why* it's built.

She is part of a growing movement of leaders who recognize that trust is not built by efficiency alone, but by inclusion, fairness, and humanity. As AI systems continue to evolve, human leaders like her will determine whether we use technology to uplift and empower, or control and divide.

ETHICAL CONSIDERATIONS IN AI-DRIVEN WORKPLACES

As AI continues to permeate every layer of organizational life, leaders face a new and urgent responsibility, navigating the ethical terrain of technology. It's no longer enough to ask whether an algorithm works, we must now ask whether it's fair, transparent, and respects the people it impacts.

Leadership in the digital age is as much about moral courage as it is about innovation.

Negotiating AI Bias and Transparency

AI systems are not neutral. They are reflections, sometimes even distorted, of the data they're trained on. When those data sets mirror existing societal biases, AI can unwittingly reinforce discrimination in critical processes like hiring, promotion, and performance evaluation.

Consider an AI that filters job applicants based on historical hiring data. If that data reflects a bias against certain demographics, the AI will perpetuate that inequality, not out of malice, but out of statistical mimicry. It doesn't know any better. That's where leadership must step in.

Leaders must act as stewards of ethical integrity, not just operational efficiency. They need to ask the hard questions: *What assumptions are embedded in this model? Whose interests does this serve? Who might it harm?* Auditing algorithms and advocating for transparency in how decisions are made is not a technical task, but a leadership imperative.

Privacy and Surveillance vs Empowerment

With AI-powered monitoring tools, organizations now have the ability to track keystrokes, screen time, movement patterns, and more. However, just because something can be measured doesn't mean it should be. There is a fine line between leveraging data for insight and crossing into surveillance that erodes trust.

Ethical leaders must draw that line thoughtfully. Productivity tracking should enable support, not enforce control. The goal is to understand workflow bottlenecks, not to micromanage behavior. Leaders must champion digital policies that prioritize employee dignity, consent, and agency.

Cultures of trust are fragile, and once broken, difficult to repair. In digital-first workplaces, leaders have to be intentional in their messaging and actions. They must ensure that technology is here to empower employees, not to stalk them. Respecting privacy is a legal and moral duty.

Reskilling, Inclusion, and the Human Cost of Tech

As automation displaces certain tasks, it simultaneously opens the door to new kinds of work. However, that opportunity isn't automatic. It requires investment in people. Leaders must resist the urge to replace and instead commit to retrain people. Reskilling is not just an HR initiative, it can be a strategic necessity and a social responsibility.

Without deliberate action, digital transformation can deepen inequality, leaving behind those without the tools or the access to adapt. Leaders must take steps to prevent a digital divide from forming within their own organizations. That means designing inclusive learning opportunities, providing mentorship, and creating upward mobility in a tech-transformed workplace.

It also means ensuring diverse voices are part of AI development and strategy. Inclusive AI is not just checking demographic boxes, it's necessary to shape systems with broader perspectives, richer empathy, and a more complete understanding of human complexity.

Real-World Example: Jim Stratton at Workday

Jim Stratton, Chief Technology Officer at Workday, says that embracing AI can elevate what makes people uniquely human, including their creativity, empathy, and ability to connect, and build a workplace where these skills drive success (*New Global Research From Workday Reveals AI Will Ignite a Human Skills Revolution*, 2025). His vision reflects a growing recognition that AI, properly guided, doesn't diminish, but amplifies humanity.

Stratton emphasizes the importance of readiness, both at the organizational and individual level. According to Workday's research, employees are not afraid of AI, but eager to engage with it, so long as it's used to enhance their potential rather than undermine it. The challenge for leaders is to build systems that support this aspiration, not stifle it.

The future of work is less centered around man versus machine. It's the fusion of machine intelligence with human wisdom. And it's leaders—human leaders—who will determine whether this fusion empowers people or replaces them.

As we conclude, one truth is startlingly clear. Technology may be transforming the *tools* of leadership, but it is not replacing the *essence* of it. That essence, rooted in empathy, judgment, ethics, and vision, remains as vital as ever. In the age of intelligent machines, the most successful leaders won't be the ones who know the most coding, they'll be the ones who know the most about people.

AI will not replace leaders, but leaders who understand and effectively harness AI will replace those who don't. As a leader, you don't have to outperform machines, but you will need to bridge the gap between what machines can and can't do. In a high-tech world, the most valuable leaders are those who bring human depth to digital environments, combining tech fluency with empathy, ethical foresight, and strategic clarity.

This new era demands more than technical competency. It calls for courage, curiosity, and a renewed commitment to the human side of work. Emotional intelligence, sound judgment, inclusive thinking, and the ability to inspire purpose are the hard edge of leadership in the age of automation.

As we move forward, the gold standard for leadership will be defined by those who can connect the dots between data and humanity, efficiency and ethics, automation and aspiration.

CALL TO ACTION

Leading forward with integrity and insight:

- **Assess your tech readiness:** Do you understand the tools your team relies on? Learn enough to lead them with clarity.
- **Develop human skills:** Make time to strengthen your emotional intelligence, communication, and moral reasoning.
- **Audit for bias:** Evaluate where and how AI is applied in your organization. Are your systems transparent and fair?

- **Champion human-centered change:** Drive reskilling, demand inclusivity in tech strategies, and ensure innovation serves people, not just performance.

The future doesn't need more machines, it needs more human leaders who know how to use them wisely.

THE RESILIENT LEADER

MASTERING GROWTH THROUGH SETBACKS

> *If you aren't making any mistakes, it's a sure sign you're playing it too safe.*
>
> — JOHN MAXWELL

Resilient leaders possess a rare capacity to navigate adversity without compromising their credibility. This chapter examines the transformative power of failure in shaping authentic leadership, offers strategies for learning from mistakes while maintaining trust, and presents practical tools to cultivate resilience in both personal and professional realms. In an unpredictable world, resilience is essential.

HOW FAILURE SHAPES STRONG LEADERSHIP

Failure has long been misunderstood in leadership. Once seen as a sign of weakness or incompetence, failure is often still stigmatized in high-stakes environments. Leaders are expected to be flawless, decisive, and constantly successful. This outdated view is not only unrealistic, it's dangerous. It prevents growth, discourages innovation, and creates cultures where people are more afraid to make mistakes than motivated to improve.

It's time to rewrite that narrative. Failure, when approached with the right mindset, becomes one of the most powerful tools for growth. Great leaders use failure to learn, recalibrate, and evolve. Reframing seeing failure as defeat to recognizing it as a necessary step in the learning process sets the foundation for resilient, emotionally intelligent leadership.

The Neuroscience of Growth After Setbacks

Modern neuroscience tells us that the brain is wired to learn from experience, especially when it involves discomfort or unexpected outcomes. This is due in large part to neuroplasticity, or the brain's ability to reorganize and form new neural connections throughout life. When leaders face failure, their brains are presented with a challenge—adapt, or stay stuck. Those who lean into the discomfort, reflect, and adjust create lasting change in their behavior and thinking patterns.

Equally important is the role of emotional regulation. Leaders who can manage the stress and emotions accompanying failure are more likely to extract meaningful lessons from the experience. They move beyond reaction and into reflection, using failure as a springboard rather than a stumbling block. This self-awareness and emotional agility become hallmarks of resilient leadership.

The Leadership Growth Curve

Leaders who experience failure, especially early in their careers, often develop deeper empathy, stronger character, and a more realistic view of the world. These individuals learn to appreciate nuance, embrace humility, and recognize the value of diverse perspectives. They understand that success isn't linear and that strength lies in persistence and adaptability.

Humility, in particular, becomes a crucial asset. Leaders who admit when they're wrong or acknowledge a misstep gain credibility. They foster trust by being human. Over time, this humility builds long-term influence and respect because people are more willing to follow leaders who can both succeed and recover with grace.

Contrast this with high performers who have never experienced failure. On paper, they may look flawless, but in practice, their leadership may falter when the inevitable challenges arise. Without the resilience built through setbacks, these leaders may struggle to navigate crises, empathize with struggling teams, or innovate under pressure. In short, experience matters, and failure is one of its greatest teachers.

Failure as an Impetus for Innovation

Failure doesn't just shape character, it drives progress. Some of the greatest innovations in history have emerged from trial and error, missteps, and "failed" attempts. In leadership, failure often highlights broken systems, inefficient processes, or outdated thinking. Leaders can open the door to what could be by confronting what didn't work.

Leaders who encourage calculated risk-taking and honest post-mortems foster a culture of continuous improvement. The goal is not to be reckless, but to be responsive. In such cultures, failures are dissected, insights emerge, and smarter strategies are the result.

Indra Nooyi's journey as CEO of PepsiCo illustrates this beautifully. During her tenure, she made bold moves that challenged traditional norms in the food and beverage industry. She prioritized long-term health and sustainability over short-term market trends—an approach that didn't sit well with all stakeholders at the time (Tellis, 2019). Her decision to shift PepsiCo toward healthier products and reimagine the company's portfolio initially faced significant criticism. Sales growth slowed, and some questioned the products. But Nooyi remained committed to her vision, understanding that the short-term dip was part of a bigger transformation. In hindsight, what some saw as "failures" were actually strategic moves that laid the groundwork for long-term success. Under her leadership, PepsiCo evolved into a more resilient and future-focused company.

Her example underscores a vital truth: Resilient leaders don't abandon vision when results waver—they adapt and hold steady. What appears to be a setback today may become the foundation of tomorrow's success.

In the end, leadership is defined by how well one responds to setbacks. True resilience lies in the ability to extract value from setbacks, to grow stronger through challenge, and to lead others through uncertainty with clarity, courage, and humility. The leaders who fail and learn are the ones who ultimately leave the most lasting impact.

LEARNING FROM MISTAKES WITHOUT DAMAGING CREDIBILITY

In today's fast-moving world, where visibility plays a high role and trust is fragile, leaders who can own their missteps and recover with integrity are respected and remembered. Let us see how.

The Anatomy of a Leadership Misstep

Even the most experienced leaders make mistakes. It's part of the territory. But not all mistakes are created equal. In leadership, they tend to fall into three main categories: strategic, interpersonal, and ethical.

A strategic misstep might involve a poor business decision, like investing heavily in an unproven market or launching a product that doesn't land. An interpersonal mistake could mean mishandling a team conflict, miscommunicating expectations, or acting with a lack of empathy. The most severe are ethical missteps, which might include breaches of trust, fairness, or organizational values.

Any of these errors can impact credibility, but how a leader handles the aftermath often matters more than the mistake itself. Leaders who ignore, deny, or deflect responsibility may preserve their ego in the short term, but they do so at the expense of trust. On the other hand, those who acknowledge and address their mistakes can actually come out stronger, gaining respect for their honesty and maturity.

Owning the Mistake: Accountability vs Defensiveness

One of the most powerful moves a leader can make after a mistake is to take full ownership, without becoming defensive or evasive. Accountability is not weakness. It's leadership in its most courageous form.

Transparency and vulnerability play key roles in repairing trust. When a leader says, "I got this wrong, and here's what I'm doing about it," they demonstrate emotional intelligence, humility, and strength. It invites others to feel safe making mistakes themselves—encouraging a culture of openness and growth rather than fear and blame.

That said, there's a fine balance between public acknowledgment and internal course correction. Not every misstep requires a public apology; the key is to assess the scope of the impact. If a decision affected your team, a department, or the broader organization, acknowledging it openly may be necessary to move forward. If the issue is internal and private, handling it directly and discreetly can be just as effective.

Knowing when to apologize and when to explain is part of a leader's emotional toolkit. A sincere apology can heal wounds. A clear explanation can provide context. But neither works without sincerity, and both lose power when coated in defensiveness. People can tell the difference between leaders who are protecting their image and those who are repairing their impact. The second type of leadership wins admiration.

Credibility Rebuilding Framework

When a mistake does cause damage to credibility, rebuilding trust requires action, and not just words. Here's a practical four-step framework leaders can follow:

1. **Acknowledge the mistake:** Be clear and specific. Avoid vague language or shifting blame. A direct "I take full responsibility for this" goes a long way in restoring faith.
2. **Take visible corrective action:** Don't just say you'll improve; show it. Make changes that can be seen and felt. Whether it's adjusting a strategy, improving a process, or mending a relationship, action speaks louder than intention.
3. **Communicate ongoing progress:** Let people know what's being done, and update them along the way. Transparency creates connection and shows you're not just moving on—you're moving forward with purpose.
4. **Reinforce integrity through consistency:** Rebuilding credibility takes time. It's not one big gesture, but a series of small, consistent choices that reestablish trust. Let your day-to-day behavior become your best apology.

Cultivating Psychological Endurance

Mistakes test strategy as well as character. Leaders need both thick skin and soft hearts. While thick skin allows you to withstand criticism, own your errors, and face discomfort without crumbling, a soft heart keeps you compassionate, self-aware, and emotionally present with those you lead.

This blend of resilience and empathy is built on emotional intelligence. Leaders with high EQ recognize their emotional triggers, manage their responses, and maintain perspective. They reflect rather than react. They learn rather than defend.

It also takes self-awareness or an honest internal check-in that says, "Where did I go wrong, and what can I learn here?" This mindset transforms failure from a scar into a stepping stone.

Ruggero Loda's story is a clear example of humility and accountability in action. As the founder of *Running Shoes Guru*, Loda once fired an employee, only to later realize he had made a mistake. Rather than bury the error or rationalize it, he took the difficult but admirable step of apologizing and mending the relationship. He publicly shared his story, acknowledging the error and what he learned from it (Rogacka & Loda, 2020). That transparency made him relatable, trustworthy, and real. His ability to admit fault, show vulnerability, and take responsibility added weight to his leadership.

Leadership only means keeping it real. It's managing tough moments with grace, learning publicly when necessary, and demonstrating that credibility doesn't come from never falling, but from always standing back up with purpose and humility.

PRACTICAL TOOLS FOR PERSONAL AND PROFESSIONAL RESILIENCE

Resilience isn't just a mindset but also a skillset. And like any skill, it needs tools, practice, and maintenance. Let us look at resilience holistically.

The Resilience Toolkit: Building the Inner Core

Like any skill, resilience needs tools, practice, and maintenance. At the heart of resilient leadership lies an inner core, a foundation built from emotional agility, self-awareness, and consistent personal habits. Leaders who maintain that core are better equipped to weather storms without losing themselves or their direction.

One of the most powerful tools for resilience is self-regulation, the ability to stay grounded in moments of pressure. Far from suppressing emotions, this means managing them wisely. Techniques like deep breathing, mental labeling ("This is stress, not failure"), and brief pauses before reacting can help leaders stay calm and present when tension runs high.

Emotional agility (David & Congleton, 2013), coined by psychologist Susan David, is another critical capability. It's the ability to experience difficult emotions like fear, shame, or frustration, without being defined by them. Leaders with emotional agility don't avoid discomfort. They move through it with curiosity, learning what it has to teach them.

Journaling is a highly underrated tool for this. A structured habit of reflection and writing down what happened, how it felt, and what one learned, can turn emotional clutter into insight. It also fosters psychological detachment, helping leaders see situations more objectively over time.

One must also not neglect the basics—sleep, exercise, nutrition, and mindfulness. More than wellness clichés, they are biological anchors. A tired brain makes impulsive decisions. A tense body holds emotional stress. Leaders who prioritize rest, movement, and moments of mental clarity build a physiological buffer against burnout and reactivity.

Bounce-Back Systems for Leaders

Every leader needs a resilience system, a personalized plan for how to recover quickly after a hit. You can think of it as a "resilience reset" or a checklist that pulls you out of emotional freefall and gets you back on track.

A sample resilience reset checklist might include:

- Step away from the problem for 15–30 minutes.
- Do a short activity that brings clarity or calm (walk, journal, meditate).
- Name the emotion you're feeling, then reframe it ("I failed" to "I'm learning").
- Reconnect with your bigger "why" to regain purpose.
- Take one small positive action like sending a message, fixing a detail, expressing appreciation.

Another effective tool is time-blocking recovery. Leaders are often so focused on productivity that they forget recovery is part of performance. After a difficult meeting, failed pitch, or emotional blow, schedule a short break or buffer time. Protecting that space helps you reset, rather than carry emotional residue into your next leadership moment.

Cognitive reframing is also essential. When something goes wrong, our inner critic often shouts first: "I messed up. I'm not cut out for this." Reframing helps shift the narrative. Instead of asking, "Why did this happen to me?" ask, "What is this trying to teach me?" Even a simple pivot such as this can transform shame into strategy.

A Resilient Team Culture Starts With You

Personal resilience is the foundation, but culture is the amplifier. The most effective leaders create environments where their teams can do the same.

This begins with modeling resilience behaviors openly. When leaders talk about their own setbacks, demonstrate healthy recovery habits, or admit they're taking a break to reset, they normalize those behaviors for others.

Creating a safe space for failure within the team is essential. You don't have to celebrate carelessness, but it does mean creating an environment where people can take smart risks, speak honestly about mistakes, and grow without fear of shame. One simple, effective practice is the "failure of the week" ritual, or a regular space where team members share something that didn't work, what they learned, and how it's helping them improve.

Embedding resilience into team rhythms through check-ins, reflection prompts, and shared wins makes it part of the team's identity, not just the leader's.

Investing in Growth After Setbacks

Finally, resilient leaders turn pain into purpose. They view setbacks not as dead ends but as doorways to greater clarity and impact. One of the best ways to leverage a setback is to invest in development through coaching, mentoring, feedback loops, and training.

Bringing in a coach or trusted advisor after a failure offers space for unpacking what happened and charting a better path forward. Mentoring others, especially after personal failure, can also transform pain into guidance, turning your experience into someone else's breakthrough.

That's exactly what Reuben Yonatan, Founder and CEO of *GetVoIP*, experienced. In pursuit of rapid success, Yonatan pushed both himself and his team too hard, leading to widespread burnout. It was a wake-up call. The short-term grind had a long-term cost. But instead of ignoring the problem, he paused, reflected, and restructured. Yonatan began to prioritize work-life balance, not just for himself, but for his entire team (Rogacka & Yonatan, 2020). He introduced new policies, adjusted expectations, and created space for recovery and sustainable performance. What began as a painful leadership lesson evolved into a more humane and resilient company culture.

His story reminds us that setbacks don't disqualify leaders. They define them. When leaders learn, adapt, and lead with empathy after failure, they become the kind of leaders people want to follow, not just during wins, but through storms.

More than bouncing back, resilience is bouncing forward. With the right tools, frameworks, and habits, leaders can transform personal struggles into platforms for stronger, wiser, and more human leadership. And in doing so, they give others permission to grow, too.

Setbacks are not detours but the curriculum of leadership. Leaders who rise after falling, and lead with both strength and vulnerability, become the ones others trust most. Remember, the true test of leadership isn't perfection, it's presence, persistence, and progress.

CALL TO ACTION

Take a moment to reflect on a recent professional setback. What did it teach you?

- Now, choose one habit like journaling, mindfulness, or a reset routine that will help you recover faster next time.
- Finally, share a personal learning moment with your team. Show them that real growth comes through imperfection, not in spite of it.

Be the leader your team deserves!

THE LEGACY MINDSET

INVESTING IN PEOPLE, NOT JUST RESULTS

> *Make a difference, change the game for the better, leave a legacy, be a guide that someone else can follow and make better, and then someone else will follow that and make that better.*
>
> — CARLOS WALLACE

In the journey of leadership, true impact is measured not just by results achieved during a leader's tenure, but by the culture they leave behind. This chapter explores the enduring influence of leadership on organizational culture —how the values, behaviors, and norms instilled by a leader shape the future long after they've moved on. Visionary leaders understand that their role extends beyond managing tasks or achieving quarterly goals; they think in terms of generations, not just fiscal years. They create a ripple effect that sustains growth, innovation, and resilience by prioritizing people, fostering a healthy culture, and intentionally developing future leaders. This chapter explores how such leaders embed purpose into everyday operations, model the values they wish to see, and invest in systems that cultivate leadership at every level. The legacy of leadership is not written in reports or headlines, but lives on in how people treat one another, how teams collaborate, and how emerging leaders carry the torch forward. As we unpack the principles of cultural legacy, we challenge readers to shift from short-term thinking to a mindset that embraces lasting impact through people-centered leadership.

CULTURE OVER OUTCOMES: THE CORE OF A LEGACY MINDSET

In today's results-driven world, leadership is too often equated with performance metrics like shareholder returns, quarterly earnings, and productivity scores. While these figures may capture a moment in time, they rarely reflect the enduring essence of leadership. Legacy has less to do with financial statements and more to do with the cultural footprint a leader leaves behind. Great leaders are remembered not for what they built, but for how they made people feel, the values they upheld, and the culture they cultivated.

Redefining success means shifting our lens from short-term outcomes to long-term impact. A leader's true influence is measured not in profits, but in people—in how they shape the everyday experience of those who carry out the mission. While transactional leaders focus on tasks and rewards, transformational leaders focus on meaning, connection, and purpose. They recognize that inspired people outperform incentivized ones over the long run. And more importantly, they understand that cultures, not campaigns, are what endure.

Culture outlives KPIs. It seeps into the language people use, the way decisions are made, and how teams respond to challenges. A campaign ends, a fiscal year closes, but culture continues to breathe through the actions and attitudes of those left behind. That's why building a strong, empowering culture isn't a side project, but the foundation of leadership legacy.

The difference between toxic and empowering cultures is stark. Toxic environments may hit short-term targets through fear, pressure, or competition, but also breed burnout, mistrust, and high employee churn. Empowering cultures, on the other hand, are built on trust, inclusion, and mutual respect. They foster psychological safety, the freedom to speak up, take risks, and innovate. Such environments make people feel better and drive better performance, lower attrition, and stronger brand loyalty.

Culture is often described as "the way we do things around here," but it's more than habits or traditions. Culture is the invisible hand that shapes decision-making, especially when no one is watching. A leader's presence may fade, but their cultural imprint lives on in the way employees treat one another, how managers lead, and how crises are handled. This unseen force determines whether a company thrives or falters once the leader is gone.

A powerful example of intentional culture-building comes from Zoom. As the company scaled rapidly during the global shift to remote work, they recognized that growth couldn't come at the cost of connection. To nurture a sense of belonging, Zoom created a "happiness crew" focused on maintaining a close-knit culture despite physical distance (*Top 15 Examples of Company Culture Done Right in 2025*, 2025). This team organizes events, checks in on team morale, and works to ensure that employees feel seen, supported, and valued. Their efforts go beyond workplace perks, they are a strategic investment in emotional well-being and cultural continuity. It's no coincidence that Zoom continues to perform strongly, both as a business and as an employer brand.

Leaders who prioritize culture understand that people are not just a means to an end; they *are* the legacy. Culture isn't a checkbox on a strategic plan; it's the very soil in which future leadership grows. When leaders invest in culture, they shape today's outcomes and secure tomorrow's possibilities.

The real question isn't whether a leader can hit the numbers. It's whether, once they're gone, the organization continues to thrive without losing its soul. That is the true mark of a legacy-minded leader.

MENTORSHIP: THE MULTIPLIER EFFECT OF GREAT LEADERSHIP

Leadership legacy is defined by who you lift up along the way. The most impactful leaders don't just build great strategies or deliver strong results; they build people. They mentor, guide, challenge, and empower others to lead. In doing so, they create a ripple effect of influence that extends well beyond their time in the role. Mentorship is one of the most powerful and enduring tools in a leader's legacy toolkit. It's how leadership DNA is passed on—not through instruction manuals, but through lived example and intentional relationships.

At its core, mentorship is more than giving advice. It's sharing perspective, providing support, and opening doors. Informal guidance, those quick hallway conversations, honest feedback moments, or quiet encouragements, often have as much impact as formal development plans. Active sponsorship, where a leader not only coaches but advocates for rising talent, helps shape the trajectory of careers and, in turn, the future of the organization. These moments, while often undocumented, embed leadership values into the culture of a team or company.

Mentorship is a multiplier. When leaders invest in one person, that person often turns around and invests in others. This ripple effect creates a self-sustaining leadership pipeline, where mentees evolve into mentors. Cultures that value mentorship see higher levels of engagement, resilience, and loyalty. Leadership development doesn't stop at the top; it radiates outward, shaping how teams communicate, collaborate, and grow.

Building mentorship into the culture of an organization requires more than encouraging one-off relationships. It calls for intentional systems. This means creating both formal structures, such as mentor-matching programs and leadership academies, and informal spaces for mentorship to thrive, like cross-functional projects or learning circles. Mentorship needs room to breathe, and also needs support and visibility from leadership.

One often overlooked but increasingly valuable approach is reverse mentorship. In this model, younger or less tenured employees mentor senior leaders, offering fresh perspectives on technology, culture, and generational shifts. It's a powerful reminder that leadership can also be reciprocal. Reverse mentorship helps senior leaders stay relevant and agile, while empowering junior talent with a sense of voice and influence.

Effective mentorship also benefits from clear frameworks. Tools like the Goal, Reality, Options, Will (GROW) model (Threadgould, 2023) or Clarify, Align, Reflect, and Empower (CARE) strategy can help structure meaningful mentoring conversations. These models ensure that mentorship goes beyond casual chatter to a purposeful process focused on development, accountability, and transformation.

The return on investment (ROI) for people development is clear. Companies that invest in leadership growth see higher innovation rates, stronger employee engagement, and lower turnover. According to research from McKinsey & Company, organizations with strong leadership pipelines are 1.5 times more likely to financially outperform their peers (*Why Leadership Development is Crucial: 5 Reasons to Invest*, 2024). Succession planning isn't just risk management—it's a strategic advantage.

Anne Mulcahy, former CEO of Xerox, is a powerful example of mentorship in action. Rising through the ranks, Mulcahy was mentored by leaders within Xerox who believed in her potential and invested in her growth. When she stepped into the CEO role during a time of deep crisis, she restructured the business to re-center it around people (Mulcahy, 2023). She prioritized leadership development, ensuring that mentorship and learning were embedded at all levels. Her approach saved Xerox from collapse and positioned the company for continued leadership beyond her tenure. Mulcahy's legacy lives on in the leaders she developed and the culture she shaped.

Ultimately, mentorship is legacy in motion, or leadership that doesn't stop at the door but continues through the lives and actions of others. Leaders who mentor well create impact, multiplying it, and in doing so, they build something that lasts.

SHAPING A LEADERSHIP LEGACY: INTENTIONAL STRATEGIES

Leaving a lasting leadership legacy doesn't happen by chance, it requires intention, clarity, and consistency. Legacy-minded leaders make decisions with the long view in mind. They don't ask themselves, "What will this achieve now?" but, "What will this mean for the culture and people five, ten, or twenty years from now?" Such leaders look beyond immediate impact. They build for sustainability. Their focus extends beyond their own tenure, aiming to cultivate trust, continuity, and principles that can withstand the test of time.

Leading for the long view means embedding resilience into both relationships and systems. It's constructing cultures and processes that don't crumble in your absence but grow stronger. Leaders who think this way prioritize transparency, psychological safety, and clear values. They understand that legacy is shaping a future that reflects the best of their leadership, even when they are no longer in the room.

A key part of legacy-building is defining your *leadership imprint*, the unique, values-driven mark you leave on an organization. This goes deeper than personal branding. While branding is how the world perceives you, legacy is how people *feel* when they work with you and what they continue to practice after you're gone. It's the difference between character and charisma. So, what do you want to be remembered for? Is it your strategic brilliance, your empathy, your belief in people, or your integrity? Legacy begins with self-awareness, knowing your values, articulating them clearly, and aligning your daily actions to reinforce them.

Identifying your leadership "signature" is part reflection, part intention. What are the consistent behaviors and beliefs that define your leadership style? Are you the leader who always listens first? The one who celebrates effort as much as results? The one who develops talent, even when it's inconvenient? These are recurring patterns that define who you are and how others experience your leadership. Over time, these patterns become the cultural touchstones that others carry forward.

Legacy is ultimately built through intentional action and repeated behaviors that reinforce what you stand for. Storytelling, as we have seen multiple times before, is a powerful legacy tool. Sharing personal experiences, company history, and lessons learned builds a shared narrative. These stories become part of the organization's cultural memory, helping guide decisions and inspire future generations.

Developing second-line leaders is another critical legacy move. Apart from leading well, you must leave behind others who can do the same. This means coaching, delegating, and providing stretch opportunities for those ready to step up. It's about creating not just successors, but stewards of the culture you've helped shape.

Legacy also lives in the artifacts you create, such as the rituals, processes, and symbols that carry meaning. These might include how meetings run, how you give feedback, or how you onboard new employees. When done with care, these everyday practices become cultural anchors or tangible expressions of your values that persist long after you've moved on.

A good example of intentional legacy-building comes from Kazuo Inamori, founder of Kyocera and KDDI in Japan (Kase, 2023). Inamori led successful companies and simultaneously built a moral framework for doing business. His philosophy, rooted in altruism, humility, and respect, was so deeply entrenched in the values of the company that it became Kyocera's leadership model. His teachings are still studied, taught, and lived by employees today. Inamori shaped a culture that remains intact decades later.

Great leadership is not measured only by how much you achieve, but by what continues to thrive after you leave. When leaders focus on people, culture, mentorship, and values, they shape something far more powerful than any quarterly result—they shape the future. Your leadership legacy is being written every day. The question is whether you are willing to write it with intention.

True leadership is measured by the lives you touch and the culture you leave behind. The most impactful leaders aren't focused on power or prestige; they invest in people. They create environments of trust, purpose, and progress. These leaders understand that legacy doesn't begin at retirement, but in the everyday. It's built through the way you listen, the opportunities you create for others, and the values you consistently uphold.

Legacy-minded leadership is not being indispensable, but empowering others to rise, even in your absence. It's not only the impact you make, but the impact you inspire in others. The question to carry with you isn't just "What did I achieve?" but "Who did I help grow?" The most powerful legacies are carried forward in the leaders who continue your work with conviction and heart.

CALL TO ACTION

You don't have to wait to start building your legacy, it can start today.

- **Identify one person you can mentor this year.** Make a commitment to invest in their growth.
- **Reflect on a core value** you want your leadership to be remembered for. Are you modeling it consistently in your actions and decisions?
- **Audit your current leadership practices.** Ask yourself honestly: If you stepped away today, would your team continue to thrive?

Legacy creation is mostly about being disciplined daily. Start now. The future is already watching.

REFLECTION AS A LEADERSHIP TOOL

THE POWER OF CONTINUOUS GROWTH

> *Average leaders raise the bar on themselves; good leaders raise the bar for others; great leaders inspire others to raise their own bar.*
>
> — ORRIN WOODWARD

Every Friday evening, after his team has logged off for the weekend, an executive at a fast-growing tech startup closes his laptop, pulls out a worn leather journal, and spends 30 minutes reviewing the week. He asks himself three simple questions: *What went well? What could I have done differently? What did I learn?*

Earlier that week, a critical product demo had gone poorly. At the moment, he had felt defensive and frustrated with his team, but he realized that he hadn't communicated the product vision clearly, and the team had been working with assumptions he never corrected.

Rather than blaming others, he acknowledged his role. The following Monday, he shared his insights with the team, honestly, without ego, and laid out a new, clearer roadmap. His vulnerability deepened trust, and his clarity refocused the team's efforts. Over time, this habit of reflection transformed him into a calm, thoughtful, and trusted leader. His decisions became more grounded, his leadership more intentional, and his team more inspired.

In a world where decisions must be made swiftly and actions carry weight, the ability to pause and reflect is often overlooked. However, it is one of the most powerful tools a leader can possess. We may think that reflection is a passive act of thinking back. In reality, it is an active, intentional process of examining experiences, thoughts, emotions, and outcomes. For leaders, reflection becomes a mirror, revealing only what has happened and who they are in the process.

This chapter explores the vital role reflection plays in shaping effective, authentic leadership. We begin by answering a fundamental question: *What does it mean to reflect as a leader?* Beyond mere introspection, it is a disciplined practice of self-awareness, accountability, and learning that sharpens insight and cultivates emotional intelligence.

We'll examine how self-awareness, the foundation of all strong leadership, grows through reflection, and how this, in turn, leads to better decision-making. Leaders who reflect are more likely to align their actions with their values, learn from failure, and adapt more quickly to change.

Reflection is a skill that can be developed. In this chapter, you'll find practical guidance and simple exercises that you can use in your daily routine to help build this critical habit. Whether you're leading a team, an organization, or yourself, reflection will help you lead with greater clarity, purpose, and impact.

Prepare to turn inward, not to retreat, but to grow.

SELF-AWARENESS: THE HIDDEN DRIVER OF EFFECTIVE LEADERSHIP

At its core, self-awareness is the ability to understand your inner world, including your emotions, values, habits, triggers, and thought patterns. For leaders, this inner clarity becomes the compass that guides decisions, shapes interactions, and sustains integrity under pressure. Without it, even the most intelligent or charismatic leader risks being reactive, inconsistent, or out of touch with their team.

Why Self-Awareness Is the Foundation of Growth

Growth in leadership doesn't begin with external skills, but from within. When leaders are aware of their strengths, they can lead with confidence. When they understand their limitations and blind spots, they become more open to learning and collaboration. Self-aware leaders welcome feedback. They know that personal insight is the seed from which professional growth blooms.

The Connection Between Inner Clarity and Outer Effectiveness

There is a direct connection between a leader's inner clarity and their ability to lead others effectively. A leader who understands their own emotional responses is far more capable of responding, rather than reacting, in high-pressure situations. This composure builds trust. A leader who knows their values makes decisions with consistency and alignment. This earns respect. Inner clarity translates into confident, decisive, and authentic leadership.

Self-Awareness Enhances Emotional Regulation, Communication, and Team Dynamics

Leaders constantly operate under emotional demands like stress, conflict, and uncertainty. Self-awareness enables emotional regulation, or the ability to notice and manage feelings without being overwhelmed or impulsive. This directly impacts how leaders communicate. A self-aware leader listens more deeply, speaks more clearly, and navigates difficult conversations with empathy.

Furthermore, self-awareness strengthens team dynamics. Leaders who understand their behavioral patterns become more attuned to those of others. They build psychologically safe environments where diverse perspectives are respected, and accountability is shared. They don't just manage, but connect with people.

Understanding Personal Triggers, Strengths, and Blind Spots

Every leader has emotional triggers, or situations that cause disproportionate reactions. For instance, some leaders may find chaos hard to deal with. Without self-awareness, these triggers can sabotage relationships and decision-making. But if recognized, they can be managed constructively.

Likewise, understanding strengths allows a leader to lean into what they do best, while identifying blind spots enables them to delegate wisely and seek complementary skills in others. Awareness can't remove flaws, but it can bring them into focus so they can be addressed thoughtfully.

Tools for Building Self-Awareness

There are many well-known tools to cultivate self-awareness:

- **360-degree feedback:** In collecting insights from colleagues, direct reports, and supervisors, leaders gain a fuller picture of how they are perceived, often revealing gaps between intention and impact.
- **Journaling and coaching:** Regular journaling helps process thoughts and emotions, while executive coaching offers a space for reflection, challenge, and insight.
- **Psychometric tools:** Instruments like the Myers-Briggs Type Indicator (MBTI), CliftonStrengths or StrengthsFinder, or EQ-i (*Myers-Briggs Overview*, 2024; *StrengthsFinder 2.0*, 2019; *What Is the EQ-i 2.0 and emotional intelligence?*, 2025) can help leaders understand their personality traits, emotional intelligence, and cognitive tendencies.
- **Mindfulness and observation:** Mindfulness practices are helpful for leaders to learn to observe thoughts and behaviors in real time, recognizing patterns that influence how they lead.

Real Life Example: Michelle Obama

Michelle Obama is a tremendous champion of self-awareness in shaping leadership. As she shared in her memoir, *Becoming*, her journey was marked by moments of deep introspection. She had to often ask herself "What do I want to do?" and "Who do I want to be?" She is often described as a leader who continually examined her motivations, questioned external expectations, and committed to leading from her values. Her ability to stay grounded, deflect criticism, and inspire millions came from knowing herself deeply and leading authentically (Soekarjo, 2019). For Michelle Obama, self-awareness wasn't a byproduct of success. It was the engine driving it.

Similarly, when leaders turn inward with curiosity and courage, they discover the clarity and resilience needed to lead outward with impact.

REFLECTIVE DECISION-MAKING: SLOWING DOWN TO MOVE FASTER

In a leadership culture that often prizes urgency, quick wins, and non-stop momentum, the idea of slowing down can feel counterintuitive, perhaps even risky. However, reflective leaders know otherwise. They understand that a strategic pause is not procrastination but precise. Reflection allows leaders to move not just quickly, but wisely.

How Reflection Enhances Strategic Thinking

Reflection gives leaders the mental space to rise above the noise of day-to-day tasks and think strategically. It creates a vantage point from which they can observe patterns, anticipate consequences, and align decisions with long-term goals. In fast-paced environments, decisions made in haste often lead to costly missteps, but when a leader takes the time to consider not just *what* needs to be done, but also *why* and *how*, the results tend to be more intentional and impactful.

This pause-before-action mindset strengthens the quality of strategic thinking. Leaders ask better questions: *Is this decision aligned with our values? What assumptions am I making? What are the potential ripple effects on people, culture, and performance?* Reflection helps leaders shift from a reactive to a proactive stance, grounded in clarity rather than urgency.

Avoiding Reactionary Decisions

In high-pressure moments, human instinct is to act quickly, fix, or react. Reaction without reflection often leads to decisions driven by emotion rather than reason. Reflective leaders use tools like post-action reviews or quiet time for analysis to assess outcomes, uncover root causes, and explore the emotional drivers behind their responses.

They examine both wins and losses to extract learning. They understand that reflection after a failed decision is critical, but so is reflecting after a success. What contributed to the positive outcome? Was it strategy, timing, luck, or people? This balanced review helps leaders refine their approach and make future decisions with more insight and agility.

Real-Life Example: Tristan Walker, Founder of Walker & Company Brands

Tristan Walker, founder of Walker & Company, makers of Bevel grooming products, is a leader who embraced reflective decision-making to gain traction in a highly competitive space (Walker, 2014; *Tristan Walker-GEM fellowship*, 2021). Early in his entrepreneurial journey, Walker was racing to keep up with the startup world's relentless pace, trying to scale quickly, attract investors, and meet the high expectations of Silicon Valley.

But after a string of missed opportunities and misaligned partnerships, Walker chose to pause. He stepped back, reconsidered his core mission, and re-centered his brand around authentic service to underserved communities, specifically black and brown men. He reshaped his company strategy, reflecting on his personal values, past decisions, and long-term vision. That moment of pause helped Walker realign with purpose and ultimately build a stronger, more resonant brand.

Reflection in Daily Leadership Scenarios

Reflection doesn't require hours of solitude. It can be built into everyday leadership moments:

- **After critical conversations**, take five minutes to jot down what went well, what felt off, and what you might do differently next time.
- **During high-pressure moments**, notice emotional responses in real-time—frustration, anxiety,

defensiveness—can prevent impulsive actions. Even a brief mental pause can shift outcomes.
- **Before delegating or initiating change,** reflecting on whether the task aligns with someone's strengths, whether the timing is right, and what the broader impact might be ensures more thoughtful execution.

In a world that is forcing us to move fast, reflection gives you a competitive edge by helping you move forward with intention, clarity, and confidence.

PRACTICING REFLECTION: SIMPLE, SUSTAINABLE HABITS FOR LEADERS

The most effective leaders integrate reflection into the rhythm of their everyday lives. They know that consistent, small practices can lead to transformation. Whether it's a few intentional minutes in the morning or a reflective team conversation at the end of the week, reflection becomes powerful when it becomes a habit.

Micro-Habits for Daily Growth

Sustainable reflection starts with micro-habits, or short, repeatable practices that fit into the realities of a busy schedule. One of the simplest and most effective is a five-minute journaling routine, either in the morning to set intentions or in the evening to process the day. Prompts such as the below can offer quick, impactful insights.

- What am I feeling and why?
- What did I learn today?

- *Where could I have shown up better?*

Another accessible method is the "What, So What, Now What?" framework:

- *What happened?* (Describe the event or situation)
- *So what?* (Why does it matter? What did you feel or notice?)
- *Now what?* (What will you do differently or carry forward?)

This method is especially useful after meetings, presentations, or key decisions—helping leaders move from experience to learning, then to action.

For broader reflection, weekly review questions can provide perspective on progress and patterns. Questions such as the following help maintain alignment with goals and values.

- *What energized me this week? What drained me?*
- *Where did I lead well? Where did I fall short?*
- *What's one insight I want to carry into next week?*

Building Reflection Into Team Culture

Reflection shouldn't just be a personal exercise, because it has the potential to transform teams when modeled and encouraged by leaders. One way to embed it into team culture is through After-Action Reviews (AARs). These short, structured conversations after projects or key events ask:

- *What was supposed to happen?*
- *What actually happened?*
- *What can we learn?*
- *What will we do next time?*

This process promotes shared learning, reduces repetitive mistakes, and cultivates psychological safety.

Leaders can also incorporate reflective questions into one-on-ones and team huddles, such as:

- *What's something you learned this week?*
- *What's one thing you'd like to improve?*
- *What's one thing that went better than expected?*

When asked consistently and with genuine interest, these questions create a culture where reflection becomes second nature.

Creating psychological safety, where people feel safe to speak openly without fear of judgment, is critical for reflective dialogue to thrive. This starts with leaders modeling vulnerability, owning their own missteps, and showing that reflection is not about blame but growth.

From Reflection to Action

Reflection without follow-through is insight without impact. The most powerful reflections lead to behavior change. This requires setting small, specific intentions based on insight. For example, one can commit to pause before responding in tense meetings or actively seeking more feedback.

Building a feedback loop, where self-reflection is paired with input from others, adds accountability and sharpens self-awareness. Whether through a coach, mentor, or trusted team member, leaders can test their internal insights against external perspectives, adjusting course as needed.

Real-Life Example: Ray Dalio

Ray Dalio, founder of Bridgewater Associates, famously said, "Pain + Reflection = Progress" (Dalio, 2019). Early in his career, Dalio lost everything after a failed market bet. He was broke and had to borrow money from his father to support his family. But rather than retreat, he reflected deeply on what went wrong and why. That painful experience shaped the radical transparency and reflective practices that now define Bridgewater's culture. Dalio credits structured reflection with helping him build one of the most successful hedge funds in history.

Ultimately, when leaders commit to small, consistent habits of reflection, they grow themselves and elevate everyone around them. As a good leader, you can't keep reacting to every problem or chase constant activity, but you can respond with clarity, intention, and self-awareness. Reflective leaders don't work harder; they work wiser. They understand that the most powerful insights don't come rushing, but in the pause. Reflection allows them to build emotional intelligence, resilience, and the capacity to learn and grow from every experience, whether it ends in success or setback.

In a world obsessed with speed and instant results, it is the thoughtful, grounded leader who will ultimately lead the future. When you take the time to reflect, you develop wisdom over and above strategies. Wisdom will allow you to move with purpose, build strong cultures, and navigate complexity with confidence.

CALL TO ACTION

Build your reflection practice:

- Start small. Commit just five minutes daily to jot down what worked, what didn't, and what you learned. Ask yourself better questions like, "How can I lead better than I did last week?" and you'll automatically start leading more intentionally.
- Create a rhythm of reflection. Pause after major meetings, high-stress conversations, or key decisions to consider your emotions, actions, and outcomes. Don't keep your insights to yourself; share them with a mentor, coach, or team member to turn reflection into accountability and collective learning.

Leadership that grows is leadership that reflects. Instead of trying to be perfect, start by being curious, because every moment you pause to reflect is a step forward in becoming the leader you were meant to be.

BRINGING IT ALL TOGETHER

YOUR ROADMAP TO IMPACTFUL LEADERSHIP

> *Before you are a leader, success is all about growing yourself. When you become a leader, success is all about growing others.*
>
> — JACK WELCH

As we have emphasized over and over, leadership is no longer confined to corner offices or titles etched on a door. In our fast-moving, interconnected world, leadership ideals have shifted. It now belongs to those who can inspire rather than command, and lead with purpose rather than power. This chapter is your bridge from insight to action.

Throughout this book, you've explored what it means to lead with empathy, communicate with clarity, and stand firm in your values while remaining agile in your thinking. You've learned true leadership is rooted in influence and not in control, and earned through trust, consistency, and emotional intelligence.

Now, as we arrive at the final chapter, it's time to bring it all together. Here, we'll distill the most essential takeaways and guide you in crafting your own roadmap for ongoing leadership growth. This is your opportunity to step beyond theory and apply what you've learned in your career, community, and personal life.

As you helm change, inspire a team, or simply strive to be a better version of yourself, the sections here will help you define your leadership identity and lead with intention.

THE LEADERSHIP SHIFT: A FINAL SYNTHESIS OF KEY LESSONS

If leadership is no longer defined by how much power you have, it's measured by the quality of your influence. The command-and-control model that once dominated boardrooms and institutions has lost its sheen in a world where complexity, interdependence, and rapid change are constants. In its place, a more nuanced, human-centered form of leadership has emerged, one that values connection over compliance, adaptability over rigidity, and collective intelligence over individual heroism.

Throughout this book, we've explored this shift in depth. Moving away from authority-based leadership, we've examined influence-based leadership. We've seen how modern leaders thrive by asking better questions, building stronger relationships, and creating space for others to grow. The arc of transformation is clear—leadership is no longer a top-down exercise in control; it is a shared, dynamic process that unfolds in context and conversation.

What distinguishes effective leadership today is not technical skills or positional titles, but key mindsets or ways of thinking and being that guide action. **Empathy** allows leaders to see others not as resources, but as people with perspectives and needs that matter. **Agility** enables leaders to respond to shifting realities without clinging to outdated plans. **Reflection** ensures that learning, both for leaders and teams, is continuous, not episodic. **Resilience** helps leaders remain grounded under pressure. **Trust-building** becomes a strategic practice, not a byproduct of success. Finally, **purpose-led decision-making** aligns short-term actions with long-term values.

In this evolving space, the leader's role has expanded beyond directing tasks. Today's leaders are connectors who bring people and ideas together across silos. They're coaches who support others in reaching their full potential. And perhaps most importantly, they are culture-shapers, intentional architects of environments where people feel safe, engaged, and inspired to contribute their best work.

This leadership model requires a critical questioning of the traditional pillars of authority. **Influence** has replaced power as the central currency. Influence is earned through **consistency, credibility, and clarity**. Leaders gain influence by creating psychological safety, where people aren't punished for speaking up or making mistakes. They practice emotional intelligence, reading situations, and responding with empathy and self-awareness. They also adapt their communication style to fit the moment, recognizing that universal messaging rarely resonates in diverse and nuanced workplaces.

Maneuvering modern leadership also means grappling with complexity. The problems leaders face today are often ambiguous and multidimensional. There are no simple formulas or fixed playbooks. Instead, resilience helps leaders stay present in the face of uncertainty, while continuous learning ensures that leaders evolve alongside the systems they serve. When you reframe mistakes as data points, growth becomes part of the culture, not just an individual pursuit.

Take the case of Hamdi Ulukaya, founder and CEO of Chobani, a real-world example of this leadership philosophy in action. His is not a traditional leadership ascent, but a story of intentional, values-driven action. Ulukaya built a successful yogurt company and redefined what a business could stand for (Ulukaya, 2022). From the start, he focused on treating his employees as owners, giving them a real stake in the company's success. He implemented inclusive hiring practices, bringing refugees and underserved communities into his workforce. He anchored every major decision in a clear sense of purpose, that business should serve people. Ulukaya's approach was a consistent application of a modern leadership mindset. He didn't have to lead with slogans, because he led with behavior. His day-to-day actions, whether on the factory floor or in executive meetings, modeled the culture he wanted to create. Over time, this built more than just a profitable company. It built a trusted brand and a loyal community of employees and customers alike.

The lesson is clear. Leadership isn't imposing control, but designing systems, behaviors, and relationships that foster trust, enable growth, and drive meaningful progress.

Authority might get compliance, but influence drives commitment. And it's commitment from teams, partners, and communities that sustains real, lasting impact.

As you move forward, consider not just what kind of leader you want to be, but what kind of culture your leadership will create. The shift is already here. The opportunity is to embody it, intentionally and unapologetically.

CREATING A PERSONALIZED ACTION PLAN FOR LEADERSHIP GROWTH

Understanding leadership as influence, resilience, and intentional culture-building is only a start. The real challenge and opportunity lie in turning insight into action. This next phase invites you to create your own personalized leadership growth plan as opposed to a rigid checklist—a living blueprint that aligns your behavior with the kind of leader you want to become.

Taking Inventory: Where Are You Now?

Before setting goals, pause to assess your current leadership style. What habits define you? What patterns show up consistently in your decisions, team interactions, or your reactions under pressure? Are you quick to offer direction but slower to listen? Do you tend to avoid conflict, or are you overly driven by performance metrics at the expense of people?

Effective leadership starts with self-awareness and honesty. Using tools like journaling, anonymous team surveys, or 360-degree feedback reviews will help you gather insight on how others experience your leadership. You might discover gaps between your intent and your impact. For example, while you may believe you encourage open communication, peers might feel hesitant to speak up in meetings. These perception gaps are golden because they show you where further growth is possible.

Identify your strengths as well. Perhaps you're deeply empathetic and create a sense of belonging, calm under pressure, or consistently clear in your vision. These are foundational strengths that can be amplified and built upon.

Designing Your Leadership Growth Blueprint

Once you've taken stock, shift to intention. What kind of leader do you want to be in the next 12 to 18 months? Choose two to three development goals that reflect the core themes explored in this book, like resilience, influence, trust, reflection, or legacy.

Let's say one goal is to become a more trust-centered leader. This might involve learning how to delegate more effectively, letting go of micromanaging tendencies, or holding regular one-on-ones focused on personal connection. A second goal could be to build resilience, not just in yourself, but in your team, by normalizing failure as a learning opportunity. This might look like running post-project reviews that ask, "What did we learn?" before asking, "What went wrong?"

For each goal, define specific actions. These could include:

- **Learning:** Enroll in a course on emotional intelligence or conflict resolution.
- **Mentoring:** Find a leadership coach or peer mentor with strengths in your growth areas.
- **Experimentation:** Pilot new habits such as starting meetings with check-ins or ending the week with reflection notes on key interactions.

Attach a timeline to each action. What will you try this week? What habit will you track over the next 90 days? What would "visible progress" look like three months from now?

Leadership growth isn't always numeric, but it should be observable. Use reflection, peer input, and behavioral outcomes to assess it. For example, improved team engagement or faster conflict resolution could be your metrics.

Making It Sustainable

The most effective leadership plans are visible in your routines. Sustainability comes from embedding small, consistent practices into your daily, weekly, and quarterly rhythms.

Daily routines could mean taking five minutes to pause and reflect on your leadership presence before a critical meeting. Weekly habits might involve scheduling one act of mentoring or feedback-seeking. Quarterly routines might involve reviewing your leadership goals and adjusting them based on what's changed in your environment, team, or mindset.

Accountability matters, too. Growth accelerates when it's not done alone. Identify a trusted coach, colleague, or mentor who can ask you hard questions, reflect your blind spots, and remind you of your commitments when you're tempted to revert to old patterns. Transparency fuels momentum.

Reflection is your reinforcement loop. Learn, apply, review, and adapt as many times as necessary. You don't have to constantly reinvent either, but consistently evolve. Leadership is a lifelong practice.

Tony Hsieh, the late CEO of Zappos, exemplified what it looks like to design and live a personal leadership roadmap (Pandey, 2023). He didn't chase traditional benchmarks of authority or performance. Instead, he committed to building a company culture rooted in happiness, autonomy, and community.

Hsieh centered his leadership on empowerment, reducing hierarchy, increasing employee ownership of decisions, and creating a workplace that felt more like a social ecosystem than a corporate machine. He wasn't afraid to challenge convention. It wasn't innovation for its own sake, but a deliberate, values-based approach supported by daily habits, personal discipline, and long-term vision.

That kind of leadership is built through deep reflection, brave experimentation, and relentless alignment with purpose.

Your Next Step

Leadership growth is pursuing alignment. Think of your action plan as a mirror. It must reflect who you are, what you value, and how you choose to show up in the spaces you influence. Take this blueprint seriously, but not rigidly. Revisit it often. Adjust it as you grow. And remember, the most transformative leaders are not the ones with all the answers, but the ones who stay curious and consistent, and lead with intention.

BECOMING A LEADER WHO THRIVES BEYOND AUTHORITY

Leadership enters its fullest expression when it transcends the need for control. At this stage, authority becomes less of a mechanism and more of a presence, earned through trust, consistency, and alignment with purpose. Leaders who thrive beyond authority cultivate environments where people step forward not because they are pushed to, but because they are inspired to contribute. Influence trumps enforcement always. It begins with letting go outdated approaches and embracing a more expansive, human-centered model.

Rejecting the Old Playbook

Traditional leadership often centered around hierarchy, compliance, and unilateral decision-making. The premise was simple: The leader held the answers, gave the orders, and maintained oversight. While efficient in predictable environments, this model restricts creativity and stifles engagement.

Thriving leaders shift from command to collaboration. They welcome diverse perspectives, invite dissent, and make decisions that consider collective input. Instead of maintaining tight control, they distribute ownership. This creates room for initiative, accountability, and genuine partnership. People grow when they're trusted. Teams thrive when they feel responsible for the outcome, not just the task.

Influence, then, becomes something cultivated through daily practice. It manifests in how leaders listen, handle uncertainty, and model vulnerability and integrity. This shift transforms leadership from a position to a presence. It builds cultures where direction emerges naturally, rooted in shared purpose.

Living Your Leadership Philosophy

At the heart of sustainable leadership is clarity of purpose. When leaders articulate their personal "why," it becomes easier to lead with intention. Your leadership philosophy should be more than a mission statement. It should be a reflection of your beliefs, values, and the impact you aim to have on the people and systems around you.

This philosophy should shape how you show up in every room, whether you're coaching a team member, navigating conflicts, or addressing a crisis. Alignment between words, actions, and values creates trust. When people see that you operate with consistency, they begin to rely on your presence and your decisions.

This alignment goes deeper than respect to create belief. When people believe in how you lead, they too begin to take ownership of their own leadership. They make better decisions, initiative, and care more.

Your Long-Term Impact

Great leaders invest in systems that extend their influence beyond their physical presence. This means developing people, shaping resilient cultures, and building processes that sustain positive outcomes. Your leadership legacy is not a final chapter; it begins now, in how you choose to lead today.

Legacy is formed in the small, repeated actions that shape how others feel, think, and act. It's present in the questions you ask, the expectations you set, and the standards you uphold. When you build trust, create opportunities, and make space for others to rise, you leave a lasting imprint that doesn't depend on your continued presence.

Eileen Fisher, founder of Eileen Fisher Inc., exemplifies this model of leadership. She designed her clothing company around ethical values, employee ownership, and collaborative decision-making (Stranahan, 2018). Over time, she stepped back from centralized control and empowered her team to lead with autonomy. Her philosophy was embedded in the company culture through shared ownership models, transparent dialogue, and an unwavering commitment to sustainability and equity.

Fisher knew that leadership ought to be embedded across the organization, not concentrated at the top. Her legacy lives in the systems she helped create that prioritize people and the planet alongside profit.

Leading Forward

Thriving beyond authority means choosing to lead in ways that outlast you. It's a form of leadership that grows stronger the more it is shared. This path requires courage—the courage to trust others, to lead with vulnerability, and to let your influence flow through action rather than command.

The work you've done through this book in reflecting, realigning, and committing to growth has positioned you to lead differently. Now, I invite you to continue that path by anchoring your leadership in purpose, presence, and trust. Live your philosophy, in building people and not just outcomes, shaping cultures and not just KPIs, and inspiring others to lead and not just follow.

In doing the above, you will become the kind of leader others aspire to be. You will make leadership safe, meaningful, and enduring.

You Are the System You Lead

Leadership today asks something deeper than strategy. It calls for presence, clarity, and personal evolution. It creates spaces for people to think boldly, speak honestly, and act with purpose. The best leaders do more than move initiatives forward. They elevate the people and systems around them through who they are and how they lead.

Your team watches more than your decisions. They watch how you show up under pressure, treat the quietest voice in the room, and consistently, your values align with your actions. In that sense, you are the system you lead. Your behavior becomes the culture's foundation. Your growth sets the pace for your team's growth and your integrity becomes the anchor others look to when navigating uncertainty.

Impactful leadership is a way of being and expressed in the questions you ask, the trust you extend, and the habits you practice daily. Evolving yourself, you shift the culture and shape systems that last. Your worth as a leader lies in making leadership more human and more effective for each one of the stakeholders.

CALL TO ACTION

Design your legacy leadership map:

- **Step 1: Reflect**—What insight from this book challenged your perspective or sparked a deeper sense of purpose? Write it down. Revisit it often.
- **Step 2: Define**—Choose two to three core values you want to embody every day, such as courage, empathy, or curiosity.
- **Step 3: Build**—For each value, create one small habit. It could be a weekly feedback check-in, a moment of reflection before key decisions, or a commitment to inclusive collaboration.
- **Step 4: Share**—Invite one trusted peer or mentor to walk this path with you. Growth accelerates in the community.

- **Step 5: Lead forward**—Choose to lead with intention. Prioritize systems that empower. Invest in people, not just performance. Let your legacy begin with how you lead today.

Leadership isn't a title. It's a practice. And it's yours to define, design, and live, starting now.

CONCLUSION

A LEADER FORGED FOR THE FUTURE

> *The ultimate measure of a man is not where he stands in moments of comfort, but where he stands at times of challenge and controversy.*
>
> — MARTIN LUTHER KING, JR.

If you've reached this point, it's likely something in you is ready for change. You might have experienced the limits of traditional leadership firsthand, seeing how control and hierarchy often fall short in real-world situations. Perhaps you've led through pressure, uncertainty, or resistance and felt there had to be a better way. Or you've recognized that a title alone doesn't earn trust, and that influence can come from any level when it's grounded in authenticity and clarity.

This book hasn't tried to give you every answer. Instead, it's asked you to slow down, reflect, and rethink what leadership actually means today and for you. Because the way people work, think, and connect has changed, leadership must change with it.

THE SHIFT IS REAL

Leadership based on authority, control, and hierarchy may still exist at organizations, but it no longer reflects how most people want to work or how the best teams operate. When people are expected to follow orders without being given reasons, it is only natural that they'll disengage. Leadership that depends on status rather than trust doesn't last long in today's environment.

You don't have to lead like that. And chances are, if you've read this far, you don't want to.

You've seen that leadership today demands different skills like the ability to build trust, communicate clearly, listen deeply, and respond with flexibility. It involves noticing the impact you have on others and taking responsibility for it, without waiting for formal permission or a perfect set of conditions.

YOU SHAPE CULTURE MORE THAN YOU REALIZE

One of the hardest and most important lessons of leadership is that people remember how you make them feel, and how you made things better or worse just by being present. The mood of a meeting, the direction of a conversation, the outcome of a tough decision can all be affected by your presence. In fact, you can convert a high-pressure situation to an opportunity.

Whether you lead a team of three or 30, whether you're part of a matrixed organization or working across silos, your words and actions set a tone. You either reinforce trust, inclusion, and learning, or make it harder for those things to take root. Leadership is lived in these small, everyday moments.

NO SINGLE FORMULA

There is no single way to lead well. What works in one environment might fail in another. The real work is understanding yourself—what you value, how you react under pressure, what blind spots you carry, and making consistent decisions based on that awareness.

This book has emphasized emotional intelligence, reflection, and resilience, not because they're trendy, but because they work. In fast-changing environments, these qualities help you stay grounded, listen better, and support others more effectively. They help you think clearly in the face of complexity and make decisions that reflect just urgency, and perhaps more importantly, integrity.

You don't need to always be certain. But you do need to be clear about what matters, what you expect, and how you plan to show up.

YOU DON'T NEED A ROLE TO LEAD

If you've ever thought, "I'm not senior enough to lead," consider this: Leadership is not a level. It's a way of working that earns respect, creates clarity, and makes things better for others and for yourself.

There are people in organizations who lead without ever being called leaders. They do it by speaking up when something doesn't make sense, supporting a colleague during conflict, and asking questions others are afraid to raise. They do it by being dependable, fair, and thoughtful in their decisions.

This kind of leadership has a real impact. It strengthens teams and shapes cultures. It often opens doors to greater responsibility, too.

YOUR LEGACY BEGINS NOW

When people hear the word "legacy," they often think about retirement or the final leg of a mission. But your leadership legacy is built now, in the choices you make each week, how you handle setbacks, and how you treat others when nobody's watching.

Ask yourself:

- *What do I want people to say about working with me?*
- *How do I want others to feel when they're around me?*
- *What would I like to be known for?*

These far-from-abstract questions point to real behaviors. You can choose to be consistent, curious, fair, and transparent. You can choose to lead conversations, build trust, and give credit. You can create a culture around you where others feel respected, seen, and encouraged to contribute.

WHAT YOU CAN DO NOW

Start with the following:

- Pick two or three leadership values that matter most to you.
- Identify one habit for each—something small you can practice every week.
- Share those values and habits with someone you trust. Let them support and challenge you.
- Take 10 minutes at the end of each week to reflect: How did I lead this week? What helped? What got in the way?

Throw out the need for perfection, but do be intentional. Leadership grows with consistent effort, honest reflection, and a willingness to adjust when something isn't working.

You've read the stories, reflected on the ideas, and explored the tools. Now comes the part that matters most—how you apply what you've learned. You have everything you need to lead beyond authority: clarity, presence, empathy, and a sense of purpose.

The next step is yours! All the best!

GLOSSARY

Adaptive communication: The skill of adjusting communication style based on audience, context, and goals. Includes managing digital communication, storytelling, and navigating hybrid environments with clarity and intention.

Adaptive leadership: A leadership style defined by flexibility, responsiveness, and the ability to lead through ambiguity. Essential in environments where standard playbooks no longer apply.

After-action review (AAR): A structured reflective practice used to analyze what worked, what didn't, and how to improve. This tool is recommended for embedding learning into team routines, especially after projects or crises.

Authoritative or top-down leadership: Leadership relying on formal roles or hierarchical control.

Contextual awareness: The ability to read the room, understand stakeholder dynamics, and tailor leadership approaches accordingly. Highlighted as essential for managing up, down, and across in matrixed organizations.

Culture-shaping: The act of actively influencing the values, behaviors, and norms of a team or organization. Leaders shape culture through modeling, language, rituals, and systems.

Empathy (in leadership): Actively understanding others' emotions and perspectives. Enhances trust, connection, and decision-making, especially during conflict or crisis.

Growth mindset: A belief that skills and intelligence can be developed through effort, feedback, and learning. Leaders are encouraged to cultivate this mindset in themselves and their teams to thrive through change.

Influence-based leadership: An approach where leaders inspire action through trust, credibility, and behavior. Influence is earned, not imposed, and is central to post-authority leadership.

The leadership trio: A set of three core competencies—**vision, resilience,** and **empathy**—that underpin all effective leadership in a changing world.

Legacy leadership: Creating lasting impact through people, culture, and systems. Encourages leaders to think long-term and design their legacy with intention.

Managing up, down, and across: A strategy for influencing in all directions—upward to senior leaders, downward to teams, and across to peers or cross-functional partners.

Multipliers: Leaders who amplify the intelligence, capacity, and creativity of those around them—as opposed to "diminishers" who suppress contribution. This idea is inspired by research referenced in the book's background sources.

Psychological safety: A team where individuals feel safe to take risks, speak up, and admit mistakes. Essential for innovation and team performance.

Purpose-led leadership: Grounding leadership in values and organizational purpose. Guides meaningful decision-making and fosters alignment beyond metrics.

Reflection loop: A continuous practice of **learn → apply → review → adapt** that builds leadership intelligence over time. Used to reinforce intentional habits and growth practices.

Resilience: The ability to recover from setbacks, manage stress, and continue leading effectively during adversity, vital for long-term leadership effectiveness.

Self-reflection: A habit of looking inward to gain insight, strengthen awareness, and improve decision-making, seen in the book as a continuous growth loop.

Shared ownership: Leadership distributed across a team, encouraging personal responsibility and mutual accountability. Increases engagement and innovation..

Storytelling (for influence): Using personal, values-based stories to build trust, convey vision, and shift mindsets. Highlighted as a communication tool that connects emotionally and builds authenticity.

Systemic change: Transformation that affects entire structures or cultures. Leaders contribute by influencing systems, not just people.

360-degree feedback: A leadership development tool where feedback is gathered from peers, direct reports, and supervisors to reveal perception gaps and uncover blind spots.

3D leadership: A model integrating **vision, values,** and **velocity** to create well-rounded, purpose-driven leadership. The book references this as a blueprint for leading in fast-moving, value-conscious environments.

Trust architecture: A framework for building and maintaining trust, based on transparency, competence, reliability, and care.

Trust Equation: A framework for building credibility: **(credibility + reliability + intimacy) / self-orientation**. Trust is seen as a measurable leadership asset.

Unscripted leadership: A leadership mindset for unpredictable contexts. Embraces emergence, iteration, and presence over rigid strategy.

Visionary thinking: Defining and communicating a compelling future. Guides teams through uncertainty and aligns actions to long-term goals.

REFERENCES

Adams, S. (2013, March 4). *10 things Sheryl Sandberg gets exactly right in "Lean In."* Forbes. https://www.forbes.com/sites/susanadams/2013/03/04/10-things-sheryl-sandberg-gets-exactly-right-in-lean-in/

Bagwe, R. (2024, September 16). *Indra Nooyi's blueprint for leadership — my notes from her masterclass.* Linkedin. https://www.linkedin.com/pulse/indra-nooyis-blueprint-leadership-my-notes-from-her-rahul-bagwe-dtkof/

Bennis, W. G., & Pham, J. M. (2023, November 6). *110 leadership quotes: Daily doses of inspiration to unlock greatness.* ITD World. https://itdworld.com/blog/leadership/leadership-quotes/#Short_Leadership_Quotes

Berg, S. (2021, November 19). *What doctors wish patients knew about decision fatigue.* American Medical Association. https://www.ama-assn.org/delivering-care/public-health/what-doctors-wish-patients-knew-about-decision-fatigue?

Bettencourt, L. A., & Brown, S. W. (1997). Contact employees: Relationships among workplace fairness, job satisfaction and prosocial service behaviors. *Journal of Retailing, 73*(1), 39–61. https://doi.org/10.1016/s0022-4359(97)90014-2

Bonaparte, N. (n.d.). *Forbes quotes: Thoughts on the business of life.* Forbes. https://www.forbes.com/quotes/6957/

Bryant, B. (2025). *Bear Bryant quote.* Quotefancy. https://quotefancy.com/quote/771436/Bear-Bryant-In-a-crisis-don-t-hide-behind-anything-or-anybody-They-re-going-to-find-you

The Career Strategist. (2024, August 5). *Transform your leadership style with Mary Barra's insights.* Medium. https://medium.com/@careerstrategist/transform-your-leadership-style-with-mary-barras-insights-e22eeb0e468f

Channell, M. (2021, October 13). *Daniel Goleman's emotional intelligence in leadership: How to improve motivation in your team.* TSW Training. https://www.tsw.co.uk/blog/leadership-and-management/daniel-goleman-emotional-intelligence/#elementor-toc__heading-anchor-2

Christman, A. (n.d.). *Empathetic leadership: Bridging division with shared common humanity.* Harvard Kennedy School. https://www.hks.harvard.

edu/centers/cpl/publications/empathetic-leadership-bridging-division-shared-common-humanity

CoFuturum GmbH. (2024, January 24). *Indra Nooyi: Charting leadership through emotional intelligence*. LinkedIn. https://www.linkedin.com/pulse/indra-nooyi-charting-leadership-through-emotional-intelligence-lrryc/

Crisis leadership and 6 effective examples of it. (2025, March 24). Doodle.com. https://doodle.com/en/resources/blog/6-examples-of-effective-crisis-leadership/

Crowley, B. (2025). *The OODA loop*. The Decision Lab. https://thedecisionlab.com/reference-guide/computer-science/the-ooda-loop?utm_

Cruth, M. (2021). *Discover the Spotify model*. Atlassian. https://www.atlassian.com/agile/agile-at-scale/spotify

Cuban, M. (2021, January 24). *Top quotes about AI, automation and robotics*. Supply Chain Today. https://www.supplychaintoday.com/ai-automation-robotics/

Dalio, R. (2019, December 4). *Billionaire Ray Dalio on his big bet that failed: "I went broke and had to borrow $4,000 from my dad."* CNBC. https://www.cnbc.com/2019/12/04/billionaire-ray-dalio-was-once-broke-and-borrowed-money-from-his-dad-to-pay-family-bills.html

Darwin, C. (2023, February 22). *50 powerful quotes on leadership for your organization*. Qualtrics. https://www.qualtrics.com/blog/50-powerful-leadership-quotes/

David, S., & Congleton, C. (2013, November). *Emotional agility*. Harvard Business Review. https://hbr.org/2013/11/emotional-agility

Dimon, J., & Spijker, N. (2024, March 12). *120+ teamwork quotes for building A strong team culture*. Rock. https://www.rock.so/blog/teamwork-quotes

Eades, J. (2021, May 11). *How great leaders make big decisions*. Learnloft. https://learnloft.com/2021/05/11/how-great-leaders-make-big-decisions/

Edmondson, A. (2014). Building a psychologically safe workplace [YouTube Video]. *TEDx Talks*. https://www.youtube.com/watch?v=LhoLuui9gX8

Esch, F. van. (2021, September 29). *The secret of Angela Merkel's extraordinary success: her understanding of the distinctive features of German politics*. The Loop. https://theloop.ecpr.eu/the-secret-of-angela-merkels-extraordinary-success-her-understanding-of-german-politics/

Ford, H., & Chakraborty, N. (2023, June 8). *50 powerful company culture quotes*. Pickcel Digital Signage. https://www.pickcel.com/blog/company-culture-quotes/

Gallo, C. (2023, July 30). *Google's CEO follows a simple public-speaking rule to deliver clear and concise messages.* Inc. https://www.inc.com/carmine-gallo/googles-ceo-follows-a-simple-public-speaking-rule-to-deliver-clear-concise-messages.html

Garratt, J., Poyton , B., & Geraghty , T. (2024, August 30). *Paul O'Neill: A psychological safety success story.* Psych Safety. https://psychsafety.com/paul-oneill-a-psychological-safety-success-story/

George, B. (2024, December 25). What Oprah's leadership journey reveals about the power of authenticity (B. Kenny, Interviewer) [Interview/Podcast]. *Harvard Business Review On Leadership / Episode 90.* https://hbr.org/podcast/2024/12/what-oprahs-leadership-journey-reveals-about-the-power-of-authenticity

Hornsby, A. N., & Love, B. C. (2020). How decisions and the desire for coherency shape subjective preferences over time. *Cognition, 200,* 104244. https://doi.org/10.1016/j.cognition.2020.104244

Howard Schultz leadership style: 5 traits to build Starbucks. (2023, December 14). San Francisco Business School. https://blog.sanfranciscobs.com/howard-schultz-leadership-style-5-traits-to-build-starbucks/

Huang, L. (2019, October 22). *When it's OK to trust your gut on a big decision.* Harvard Business Review. https://hbr.org/2019/10/when-its-ok-to-trust-your-gut-on-a-big-decision

Ignatius, A. (2021, November 5). *Indra Nooyi, former CEO of Pepsico, on nurturing talent in turbulent times.* Harvard Business Review. https://hbr.org/2021/11/indra-nooyi-former-ceo-of-pepsico-on-nurturing-talent-in-turbulent-times

Jeff Bezos. (2023, January 17). Renaissance Marketer. https://renaissancemarketer.com/list/jeff-bezos/

J S, S. (2024, January 23). *How Apple uses empathy in design and wins customers' hearts! (Part 2: AutoFill OTP, airdrop, privacy features).* Medium. https://medium.com/@shreyasjswork/how-apple-uses-empathy-in-design-and-wins-customers-hearts-4a1c7edd7be4

Kase, K. (2023, February 22). *Inamori management philosophy: putting faith in employees.* IESE Insight. https://www.iese.edu/insight/articles/inamori-management-philosophy-imp-book/

Kelly, S. (2024, September 5). *Microsoft is turning to AI to make its workplace more inclusive.* BBC. https://www.bbc.com/worklife/article/20240905-microsoft-ai-interview-bbc-executive-lounge

King Jr., M. L. (1963, August 28). "I Have a Dream" Speech, in Its Entirety. Talk of the Nation [Radio]. *NPR*. https://www.npr.org/2010/01/18/122701268/i-have-a-dream-speech-in-its-entirety

King, Jr., M. L., & Walter, E. (2013, September 30). *50 heavyweight leadership quotes*. Forbes. https://www.forbes.com/sites/ekaterinawalter/2013/09/30/50-heavyweight-leadership-quotes/

Kraut, R. (2025, March 21). *Socratic method*. Encyclopedia Britannica. https://www.britannica.com/topic/Socratic-method

Kruse, K. (2019, June 10). *52 quotes about trust and leadership*. ConantLeadership. https://conantleadership.com/52-quotes-about-trust-and-leadership/

Loonam, M. (2024, December 13). *Leadership lessons, Steve Jobs-style*. Arizona State University: W. P. Carey News. https://news.wpcarey.asu.edu/20241213-leadership-lessons-steve-jobs-style

Macpherson, L. (2021, February 5). *8 examples of transparent leaders to follow*. Front. https://front.com/blog/8-examples-of-transparent-leaders-to-follow

Maxwell, J. (2024). *60 self-development quotes to inspire and enlighten you*. Indeed Career Guide. https://ca.indeed.com/career-advice/career-development/self-development-quotes

Mcgirt, E. (2020, March 23). *Marriott CEO's authentic message to employees*. Fortune. https://fortune.com/2020/03/23/marriott-ceos-authentic-message-to-employees/

Meier, J. (2024, December 28). *Leadership lessons from Satya Nadella*. JD Meier. https://jdmeier.com/leadership-lessons-from-satya-nadella/

A message from co-founder and CEO Brian Chesky. (2020, May 5). Airbnb Newsroom. https://news.airbnb.com/a-message-from-co-founder-and-ceo-brian-chesky/

Mulcahy, A. (2023, December 11). How Anne Mulcahy turned Xerox around – and what came after (R. Gulati, Interviewer) [Podcast Interview]. Deep Purpose. *Harvard Business School*. https://www.hbs.edu/news/podcasts/deep-purpose/Pages/podcast-details.aspx?episode=4563078396

Munn, B. (2013). *Nelson Mandela's servant leadership: What we can learn from him*. Billmunncoaching.com. https://billmunncoaching.com/nelson-mandela-servant-leader/

Myers-Briggs overview. (2024). Myers & Briggs Foundation. https://www.myersbriggs.org/my-mbti-personality-type/myers-briggs-overview/

Nadella, S. (2021, October 28). Microsoft's Satya Nadella on flexible work, the metaverse, and the power of empathy (A. Ignatius, Interviewer)

[Interview]. In *Harvard Business Review*. https://hbr.org/2021/10/microsofts-satya-nadella-on-flexible-work-the-metaverse-and-the-power-of-empathy.

Nakanishi, D. S. (2025). Adaptation studies on Netflix: Approaches for theorizing streaming platforms. *Ilha Do Desterro, 77*, e98153. https://doi.org/10.5007/2175-8026.2024.e98153

New global research from Workday reveals AI will ignite a human skills revolution. (2025). Newsroom | Workday. https://newsroom.workday.com/2025-01-14-New-Global-Research-from-Workday-Reveals-AI-Will-Ignite-a-Human-Skills-Revolution

O'neill, B. (2024, April 9). *The downfall of Uber's co-founder and CEO Travis Kalanick.* Sunrise Geek. https://www.sunrisegeek.com/post/the-downfall-of-ubers-co-founder-and-ceo-travis-kalanick

Panayides, J. (2024, September 18). *Measuring what matters: The role of psychological safety metrics in HR.* MyHRfuture. https://www.myhrfuture.com/blog/measuring-what-matters-the-role-of-psychological-safety-metrics-in-hr

Pandey, V. (2023, May 24). *The Zappos model: How delivering happiness transforms business and leadership.* LinkedIn. https://www.linkedin.com/pulse/zappos-model-how-delivering-happiness-transforms-business-pandey/

Pappas, C. (2025, March 31). *30+ surprising leadership statistics to take note of.* ELearning Industry. https://elearningindustry.com/surprising-leadership-statistics-to-take-note-of

Poyton, B. (2024, March 28). *Google's Project Aristotle.* Psych Safety. https://psychsafety.com/googles-project-aristotle/

Rampen, J. (2019, April 12). *How Tim Cook has used Apple to turn diversity into a priority for tech firms.* DiversityQ. https://diversityq.com/how-tim-cook-has-used-apple-to-turn-diversity-into-a-priority-for-tech-firms/

Richman, J. (2016, May 27). *5 Examples of Companies Succeeding Through Transparency.* Entrepreneur. https://www.entrepreneur.com/growing-a-business/5-examples-of-companies-succeeding-through-transparency/274636

Rodriguez, A. (2018, April 14). *As Netflix turns 20, let's revisit its biggest blunder.* Quartz. https://qz.com/1245107/as-netflix-turns-20-lets-revisit-its-biggest-blunder

Rogacka, O., & Loda, R. (2020, August 27). *12 leadership stories: Mistakes and lessons learned: #4 Making important decisions based on emotions.* LiveChat. https://www.livechat.com/success/stories-from-leaders-mistakes-lessons-learned/

Rogacka, O., & Yonatan, R. (2020, August 27). *12 leadership stories: Mistakes and lessons learned: #10 pushing too hard.* LiveChat. https://www.livechat.com/success/stories-from-leaders-mistakes-lessons-learned/

Sandberg, S. (2011, October 5). Facebook's Sheryl Sandberg on what makes women succeed (P. Sellers, Interviewer & M. Barnett, Author) [Interview]. *Fortune.* https://fortune.com/2011/10/05/facebooks-sheryl-sandberg-on-what-makes-women-succeed/

Satya Nadella's Transformation of Microsoft. (2024, September 2). Humans of Globe. https://humansofglobe.com/satya-nadellas-transformation-of-microsoft/

Schmidt, L. (2019, August 21). *Why HubSpot treats its culture as a product—and how that helps them attract great candidates.* LinkedIn. https://www.linkedin.com/business/talent/blog/talent-engagement/why-hubspot-treats-culture-as-product-to-attract-candidates

Schultz, H. (2010, July 1). The HBR interview: "We had to own the mistakes" (A. Ignatius, Interviewer) [Interview]. *Harvard Business Review.* https://hbr.org/2010/07/the-hbr-interview-we-had-to-own-the-mistakes

Sean McPheat. (2024, March 20). *Exploring Barack Obama's leadership style.* MTD Training. https://www.mtdtraining.com/blog/barack-obama-leadership-style.htm

Semuels, A. (2024, March 31). *Why Chanel CEO Leena Nair is leading with compassion.* TIME. https://time.com/6962053/leena-nair-chanel-interview/

Shaw, G. B. (2020, July 8). *Leadership quotes about communication.* Nally Ventures Leadership. https://www.nallyventuresleadership.com/2020/07/07/leadership-quotes-of-the-week/

Sinha, S. (2023, March 24). *IBM: From hardware to software to quantum computing (A brief study).* Medium. https://swaysinha.medium.com/ibm-from-hardware-to-software-to-quantum-computing-a-brief-study-2d1d8eb956e4

Soekarjo, M. (2019, April 24). *Five lessons from Michelle Obama on becoming your authentic self.* LinkedIn. http://linkedin.com/pulse/five-lessons-from-michelle-obama-becoming-your-self-mara-soekarjo/

Stranahan, S. (2018, August 16). *Eileen Fisher: Designing for change.* Medium; Fifty By Fifty: Employee Ownership News. https://medium.com/fifty-by-fifty/eileen-fisher-designing-for-change-f6877b4130f1

StrengthsFinder 2.0. (2019). Gallup.com. https://www.gallup.com/cliftonstrengths/en/254033/strengthsfinder.aspx

REFERENCES | 241

Taplin, S. (2024). Leadership Evolution: Inspiration from Elon Musk and Mark Cuban. *Forbes*. https://www.forbes.com/councils/forbestechcouncil/2024/05/06/leadership-evolution-inspiration-from-elon-musk-and-mark-cuban/

Tellis, S. (2019, October 3). *How Indra Nooyi got PepsiCo's customers to accept a heart-healthy alternative to potato chips*. The Economic Times. https://economictimes.indiatimes.com/magazines/panache/how-indra-nooyi-got-pepsicos-customers-to-accept-a-heart-healthy-alternative-to-potato-chips/articleshow/71419259.cms?from=mdr

Thaken, M. (2023, November 10). *Women in leadership | Sheryl Sandberg*. Medium. https://manasi-thaken.medium.com/women-in-leadership-sheryl-sandberg-2e5c249adb55

Threadgould, M. V. (2023, June 10). *What Is the GROW Coaching Model?* Lattice. https://lattice.com/articles/everything-you-need-to-know-about-the-grow-coaching-model

Titov, M. (2024, July 30). *Key elements of Spotify's agile scaling model*. Altigee Magazine. https://www.altigee.com/magazine/spotify-agile-model-elements-principles-and-takeaways

Top 15 examples of company culture done right in 2025. (2025, February 13). Vantage Circle. https://www.vantagecircle.com/en/blog/examples-of-company-culture/#8-a-hrefhttpszoomus-targetblank-relnofollow-zoom-a

Tristan Walker - GEM fellowship. (2021, August 12). GEM Fellowship. https://www.gemfellowship.org/teams/tristan-walker/

The trust equation: A simple summary. (2019, July 8). The World of Work Project. https://worldofwork.io/2019/07/the-trust-equation/

Ulukaya, H. (2022, April 26). Chobani founder Hamdi Ulukaya on the journey from abandoned factory to yogurt powerhouse (A. Ignatius, Interviewer) [Interview]. In *Harvard Business Review*. https://hbr.org/2022/04/chobani-founder-hamdi-ulukaya-on-the-journey-from-abandoned-factory-to-yogurt-powerhouse

VanderLinden, S. (2024, October 31). *What are Patagonia's sustainability practices: Key initiatives and impacts*. Medium. https://medium.com/@sabine_vdl/what-are-patagonias-sustainability-practices-key-initiatives-and-impacts-81e821fe6d68

Walker, T. (2014, December 15). Tristan Walker: You should always ask, "What if?" (E. B. Ekiel, Interviewer) [Interview]. *Stanford Graduate School of Business*. https://www.gsb.stanford.edu/insights/tristan-walker-you-should-always-ask-what-if

Wallace, C. (2025). *Legacy quotes (390 quotes)*. Goodreads. https://www.goodreads.com/quotes/tag/legacy-quotes

Walton, S. (2022, June 25). *62 inspirational manager quotes*. Indeed Career Guide. https://www.indeed.com/career-advice/career-development/manager-quote

Welch, J., & Walter, E. (2013, September 30). *50 heavyweight leadership quotes*. Forbes. https://www.forbes.com/sites/ekaterinawalter/2013/09/30/50-heavyweight-leadership-quotes/

What Is the EQ-i 2.0 and emotional intelligence? (2025). EITC. https://www.eitrainingcompany.com/eq-i/

Why leadership development is crucial: 5 reasons to invest. (2024, July 11). High Performance Leaders. https://hp-leaders.com/blog/why-leadership-development-is-crucial-5-reasons-to-invest

Woodward, O., & Belknap, L. (2025). *50 inspirational leadership quotes*. Ethos3. https://ethos3.com/50-inspirational-leadership-quotes/

Wright, G., & Wigmore, I. (2022, May). *What is VUCA (volatility, uncertainty, complexity and ambiguity)?* TechTarget https://www.techtarget.com/whatis/definition/VUCA-volatility-uncertainty-complexity-and-ambiguity

Yolga, B. (2023, November 16). *How warehouse automation is revolutionizing Amazon logistics*. Carbon6. https://www.carbon6.io/blog/how-warehouse-automation-is-revolutionizing-amazon-logistics/

Zainuddin, S., & Isa, C. R. (2019). Workplace fairness, information sharing and employee performance in a budget setting: an empirical study. *Gadjah Mada International Journal of Business, 21*(2), 135. https://doi.org/10.22146/gamaijb.31133

ABOUT THE AUTHOR

Nakel Nikiema is a psychologist, management expert, author, and consultant specializing in business intelligence, governance, and decision-making. With over 20 years of experience in global organizations like the United Nations Millennium Campaigns, NORC at the University of Chicago, and ORBIS Charitable Trust, he has seen firsthand how data can shape—or mislead—critical decisions. Born in Burkina Faso, Nakel's international background and leadership roles give him a unique perspective on data use, strategy, and organizational growth. His books cover topics such as artificial intelligence, finance, and Africa's development, always aiming to provide practical, real-world insights. Beyond writing, Nakel works as a mentor and consultant, helping businesses and leaders navigate data-driven decisions with clarity and confidence. Through his work, he strives to equip others with the knowledge they need to make smarter, more informed choices.

www.ingramcontent.com/pod-product-compliance
Lightning Source LLC
Chambersburg PA
CBHW050246010526
44107CB00003B/201